The Burial Brothers

The Burial Brothers

Simon Mayle

The Ballantine Publishing Group • New York

A Ballantine Book
Published by The Ballantine Publishing Group

Originally published in Great Britain by Hamish Hamilton Ltd., in 1996.

http://www.randomhouse.com

Library of Congress Catalog Card Number: 97-97068

ISBN: 0-345-41357-1

This edition published by arrangement with Grove-Atlantic Inc.

Manufactured in the United States of America

Cover design by Min Choi
Cover photo © Michael A. Barruzza/Professional Car Society

First Ballantine Books Edition: January 1998

10 9 8 7 6 5 4 3 2 1

For Pops

I

It was on page 47 of *Buyer's Weekly*, in the Cadillac section, next to an advertisement that read, 'Coupe de Ville. $3000. He's gone, so can his car': a small blurred black-and-white shot of a large black automobile. Underneath were the words: 'Hearse. Cadillac. 1973. 31,000 miles. Cruise-Control. V8. Garaged. Only two owners. $3500. Immaculate.'

It was the only hearse for sale that week in *Buyer's Weekly*, would probably be the only hearse for sale in the paper for months to come, but there it was on page 47 with a smudged picture and a short but informative description.

I read the advertisement again. The price was good. The mileage was low considering the car was twenty years old. The body looked clean. It had an impressive set of perform-ance fins, wheelskirts, chrome trim, whitewall tires, and a symbol on the coachwork common to every hearse every-where in the world: the slanting *f*. This *f* was most important. With it clearly visible on the coachwork there could be no confusing this automobile with the average family wagon. Where I wanted to go this was important.

The number listed was 718, the Queens borough of New York City. I called. An old lady answered. I told her I was calling about the car in the paper, the 'seventy-three hearse, was it sold?

'Sold?' She laughed. 'No. No, it's not sold. In fact, you're the first caller he's had all week.'

'That's good,' I said.

'Not for him it ain't,' she replied.

I left my number and asked if the owner could call me when he had a chance. Then I called Potamkin Cadillac. Potamkin Cadillac are advertised as New York City's leading Cadillac dealer. I spoke to a man in sales. A mint 'seventy-three hearse, I asked him, what would be the market value on one of them these days? The salesman laughed. He asked me why I wanted to know. When I explained things, he was most helpful indeed. Depending on condition and mileage, $3500 was a fair price. That's what he said. I thanked him and put the phone down.

A little while later I spoke to the owner, a man called Tony. I asked Tony to tell me a little more about this hearse of his.

'Twenty-one feet in length. Two-and-a-half tons in weight. Nine-and-a-half liter V8 General Motors engine. Only two owners, myself and a funeral service out in Jersey. This car is beautiful, my friend, bee-utiful.'

'I want to come see it.'

'When?'

'As soon as possible.'

He gave me the address of his mother out in Astoria and told me to come by at two the next afternoon. 'By the way,' he added, 'you in the business?'

'The funeral business?'

'Yeah.'

'No.'

'Me neither. Antiques. See you tomorrow.'

I put the phone down. The rest of that day passed slowly. On the news they said the subway system out to Jersey was flooded. Later they amended that report: the subway system out to Jersey *and* Brooklyn was flooded. The worst winter in decades was about to hit the city. That's what the weathermen opined. All in all it was a very good time to be leaving.

Two the next afternoon I arrived promptly in Astoria to meet Tony. Tony was a short man; heavy, thick black hair, gold necklace, gold wrist-band, gold watch, dressed in black.

'You the guy who wants to see the car?'

'That's me.'

He smiled. 'Before we start this I want you to understand, I don't do no deals. You want my car, you pay the price in full. Capisci?'

I shrugged.

'Good enough. Follow me, please.'

Five minutes later we were walking down the street and Tony was giving me a short, detailed account of his brief involvement with the car. It brought a big smile to my face. His reasons for selling were unique. It wasn't that he *wanted* to sell. He didn't. But he *had* to. It was, he said, a matter of simple economics.

'It comes down like this. I keep my three-and-a-half-thousand-dollar car. Or, I keep my two-hundred-and-twenty-five-thousand-dollar condo.'

The story went like this. Tony had just moved into a luxury condominium complex out on Long Island. It was a beautiful place, prime real estate, doorman, health club, but it had cost him $225,000 to buy. He'd been there only three weeks when the neighbors started.

'They didn't say the problem was the type of car, you understand? They said it was the length. At twenty-one feet – fucking pricks measured it, I watched 'em do it – at twenty-one feet in length they said the car violated the local parking codes, so it had to go. But you know what? That's a crock of shit, my friend. The truth is these people are old and scared and they don't like lookin' out their living-room windows at night to be reminded that their tenancy at the Forest Glades Luxury Condominium Complex is temporary not permanent. But that's what it is. My three-and-a-half-thousand-dollar hearse or my two-hundred-and-twenty-five-thousand-dollar condo. Like I said, a matter of simple economics.'

So the hearse upset people. This was good.

'I'm looking forward to seeing it,' I said.

'You can't miss it, pal,' said Tony.

We turned a corner. Then I saw the car for the first time. Taking up two whole parking spots, the length of a stretch limousine, about six or seven feet wide, an incredible piece of automotive hardware.

'So,' Tony asked me, 'you like it, pal?'

'It's beautiful, Tony.'

'So take a walk around. Anything I can help you with, just ask, a'right? I'm here to help.'

Tony lit a King Size menthol cigarette, then leaned up against the front deck of the car. I circled the machine slowly. It was exactly as it had been represented in the paper: immaculate. The paintwork was raven-black, the chrome was polished, there were no dings, no dents, no rust, the white-walls were spotless and yet he was only asking $3500. It was a steal.

'What's under the hood?'

Tony unlocked the driver's door, reached inside to pull the hood release and it popped with a dull thud. I hooked my fingers through the large grill, released the catch, then lifted. The hood sprang open on heavy springs. It was enormous.

Tony turned it over. The motor fired first time. Everything looked clean and orderly. I banged the hood down.

'That all you want to see?' Tony asked me.

If this had been any other brand of automobile, I would have taken an expert with me out to Queens that afternoon. But I had this theory that dollar-for-mile the hearse had to be the most mechanically sound and economically irresistible car good borrowed money could buy. The 31,000 on the clock would be original miles (how far is it going to be from funeral home to cemetery and back, five times a week, fifty-two weeks of the year, even over twenty years?). 31,000 is nothing for a 472 V8. Also, as everyone knows, a hearse probably never tops out at more than thirty during its working career. At thirty m.p.h. the only thing you're likely to strain is the patience of the man sitting in the car behind you. Then there's the original owner to consider. A professional man. Someone whose livelihood *depends* on his automobile's reliability. Any smart undertaker is going to have the car serviced at the correct interval, make sure it never suffers from rust, and – a big bonus here – never let junior take the car out to pull donuts and tranny drops while picking drag races with his pals on Friday night, something I fondly remember doing with my brothers when opportunity presented itself. With all of this on the table I felt confident this old hearse was going to sing like a bird and pull like a train, and that's why I pushed the hood down and asked to see the automobile's interior. I did not feel an obligation to explain this to Tony. He was in a hurry and didn't ask, anyway.

This machine was going to be home for the next six weeks. As such there were certain needs which had to be inspected before handing over money. It had to be big enough for a bed, for example. It had to *look* like a hearse. And it had to have a good set of curtains.

Tony opened up the rear door. I peered inside. The interior was cavernous. Divided into two compartments, the staff area was up-front, the client quarters in the rear. However, the first thing you noticed when you swung open the rear door were the rollers. Eight of them, embedded in a fake walnut floor, arranged in two lines, to ease extraction of the coffin.

'Can take a nine-footer, no problem,' Tony said. 'That's what I was told.'

I climbed in, turned around, then stretched out. It had three plain glass windows in the three doors – two at the sides, one at the rear. It had a bathtub ceiling. Three light fixtures scalloped on the walls. Black naugahyde wall finishing – but there were no curtains.

'Tony?'

He was looking across the street at a pretty young mother pushing her child.

'What?'

'You have curtains?'

'The fuck do I need curtains for?'

I crawled out.

'I need curtains.'

Tony shrugged. Then he shot his cuffs and tapped the glass of his gold watch. 'We gotta get movin' here, pal. I got a lotta business to take care of this afternoon.'

So we went for a test drive. I sat in the front on the long bench-seat, Tony drove. Tony wouldn't let me drive. I didn't care anyway. At this point I was more interested in seeing what was going on *around* the car, not *in* it.

After a ten-minute ride around Queens, I was a proselyte.

People stopped and stared. Kids pointed. One little old lady made the sign of the cross and hurried off. All this respect. And we weren't even armed. When we pulled up to the curb, I told Tony I wanted it.

'A wise decision, my friend,' he said. 'You won't regret it.'

'But there is one thing that troubles me, Tony.'

'What?'

'I need curtains.'

Tony sighed. 'What kinda curtains were you thinkin'?'

'I don't know. Velvet might be nice.'

'*Velvet?*'

We argued about this. In the end Tony dropped his price fifty bucks. I counted this as a small victory. I paid the balance in cash, he gave me a bill of sale, the title of the vehicle, and the keys. I now owned a hearse. It was my first automobile.

People often say cars are a reflection of their owner's ego. Successful businessmen buy expensive German cars. Young studs race around in large-capacity performance cars. Ladies like the convertibles. So what, I wondered as I headed back over the Williamsburg Bridge to Manhattan in the late-afternoon traffic, did this hearse have to say about the state of mine? Dead? Or just getting started? I believe it was Ambrose Bierce who said about hearses they're death's baby carriage. But maybe old Ambrose meant play-pen.

2

There is an old saying that goes something like, 'When the going gets tough, the tough run away on holiday.' That's what I was doing. I was going down to the other end of the planet, where at this time of the year – we were coming into the Christmas holidays in America – it was summer.

Every year in Rio they have a big party on the beach called carnaval. Carnaval is a one-week hoolie where the whole of Latin America gets pie-eyed. Carnaval seemed to me to be a just and fitting reward for a long, perilous overland road trip. Carnaval was the other side of fifteen thousand miles, thirteen frontiers, two or three war zones, two tropics, the equator and the mighty Andes. All of it to get through. In about six weeks. In an old hearse. I did not anticipate any problems with this.

A run like this, however, is not something you want to get into on your own. First, because you can have a *lot* more fun if you travel in company. Second, because as my wise old grandmother pointed out, it's always better if there are *two* of you getting into trouble because then there's *twice* the chance someone will come and look for you. Some of these places were very dangerous. They also happened to be very cheap. One of the reasons they were very cheap was because they were very dangerous. And so on. However, it's not easy finding somebody else to drive with to Brazil. People are a little hesitant about dropping everything and running off for a couple of months in a big old funeral car to countries with a worse human rights record than the Los Angeles Police Department. There are a variety of reasons for this, but personal safety seems to be the most popular. There was one man, though, I knew I could call in a time of need; an old friend, well traveled, who happened to live on a farm on the north coast of Cornwall, over in England. His name was Tarris Hill and I had known the bugger for over ten years. I rung him up a little before Christmas with an invitation to join me on this party run.

His reply was simple and predictable: 'When we leavin', bunje?'

He said he was very glad that I had called, because life had been getting just a little dull recently. He was up for a little sport. Besides, he added, going down to South America would be an ideal opportunity to seek out exciting new business opportunities. Tarris was a wheeler/dealer.

'Like what?' I asked.

'Import/export.'

'Import/export what?'

'Ah. That's what I will find out.'

He was an ideal companion; a roughneck; half his life had been spent working in oil camps in the Third World, he knew how things *worked* down there. I was a novice tourist. Once, I had been to the Yucatan. Tarris would be a valuable man to have in the corner. The only problem was this: he refused to come to New York and there was nothing I could say that would persuade him to do otherwise. He'd be happy to meet somewhere like Honduras, but *not* the United States. He'd driven through it, didn't want to drive through it again.

This, of course, was a minor set-back. I didn't want to drive down to Honduras on my own. In fact I didn't want to drive to exit 7 on the N. J. Turnpike on my own. Honduras is the other side of Guatemala; in Guatemala they are having a civil war, and have been for years. I called friends. I called friends of friends. Nobody wanted or could come along. And that's when I met Lenny . . .

It was at a little Christmas gathering in a loft downtown. The minute I walked in I noticed him standing in the middle of the room, pants held up with twine, wearing a dirty overcoat, a stained felt hat and an old pair of scuffed black workboots. He was clearly an Artist. About thirty, large build, a man who could flit between the soup lines on the Bowery and the gallery openings in SoHo with ease. The hostess introduced me.

'Have you met Lenny?'

'No.'

'No? Oh well, you just *have* to meet Lenny,' she said. 'He's a riot! You'll love him!'

So I was taken over and reluctantly introduced soon after. The hostess told him I was going away on a trip.

'How nice,' he said caustically. 'Where you going?'

'Brazil,' I said.

'Well, it sure is lucky for some, *isn't* it?'

'Lenny,' said our hostess. 'Be nice. He's not flying, he's *driving*!'

An eyebrow lifted. He found this almost interesting. Almost.

'To Brazil?'

'Next week.'

'You need company?'

And that, more or less, is how we came to be traveling together. A lot later he told me how he came to be in a position to ask me for a ride. The story went like this: two nights earlier Lenny and his wife of three years had a fight. Not a big fight, just another fight, one of many they had been having with increasing frequency. Lenny flees the house, goes to a party in Chinatown. When it comes time to leave this party and go home he realizes he hasn't got enough in his pockets to pay for a cab. It's too far and too cold to walk. All his friends and acquaintances from whom he could have borrowed money have left, so he has no choice but to take the subway. He bundles up against the cold, heads out on to the empty street and roams around downtown until he finds an open subway. By this time, however, it's around three o'clock in the morning and Lenny is sliding fast. It's been a long, emotionally fraught day. He wants to get home and get to bed. He goes into the station, descends to the eastbound platform, collapses on a bench and waits. The train takes forever to arrive. By the time it pulls into the station, Lenny can't keep his eyes open another second. He stumbles aboard. The carriage is empty. He slumps in a seat. Soon he is fast asleep, which is quite a feat because seats on the New York subway are not comfortable. All night long Lenny sleeps on this train as it rattles in and out of Manhattan going through some of the nastiest, most violent neighborhoods in the city. And here's the extraordinary part – nobody touches him. Not once in three circuits of the South Bronx. Eight the next morning Lenny is woken violently but he quickly deduces he's not in mortal danger. A woman is doing the shaking and she is an old soldier from the Salvation Army. He asks this old lady what she thinks she's doing waking him up, frightening him half to death like that. She waves a dollar bill in front of his runny nose. 'Here!' she brays. 'It's only a dollar but you sure look like you could use it!'

This is a most horrible shock first thing in the morning. But at least the old woman is trying to *give* him money, not take money *away* from him. A good start. He asks her what time it is. Eight-fifteen. Then he remembers: eight-fifteen! He's meant to be at work at eight-thirty! That means he has fifteen minutes to get from wherever he is to the SoHo district of New York City. But where exactly is he?

Lenny asks the old lady. She tells him he's in the Bronx. Anywhere in the Bronx is a couple of connections and maybe thirty minutes from SoHo. Lenny is not going to make eight-thirty. In fact, he's going to be lucky to make nine o'clock. He jumps off the train, jumps on the next train heading back to Manhattan, and forty-five minutes later rolls into work out of breath, penitent, sweating, but full of gorgeous apologies. The boss is not amused. She had to hire some guy off the street to help bring in a new shipment and the guy tried to walk off with one of her paintings.

A quick assessment of the damage and Lenny realizes he is in the soup. He compliments her on her hair, her clothes, her teeth (she's just spent $40,000 on bridge-work) – none of it works. Her face is red, unappeasable and fractious. The only thing that can save him is the truth. She's a nice little JAP from the Upper East Side – she might be amused by his quaint beatnik behavior. She's not. She fires him. Lenny clutches at her new $2000 Prada outfit and says, 'It's Christmas, Miss Schwartz. You can't fire a man a week before the Christmas holidays. Shit, what about Peace, Love and Understanding . . .? What about one last chance?' But Miss Schwartz says she gave him one last chance four last chances ago, beat it!

Lenny is stunned. This isn't the first time this kind of thing has happened in his life. It's happened before, many times as a matter of fact, but at this time of the year the cruel hand of fate has dealt him a vicious blow. One way of looking at it. But it will free up his time and allow him to paint, which, as an artist, is something he must do. Another way of looking at it.

Lenny turns on his worn heels. It's a sad end to a useful

spell of employment. He hops on a subway car at Prince and heads back to Brooklyn, managing to retain a surprisingly balanced and philosophical outlook on it all. Maybe that scrawny, neurotic, sushi-eating bitch will drop dead, he thinks. Maybe not. One can only live in hope. In the meantime, he hasn't seen or talked to his wife since he left the house the night before, and he has to sort things out. The only sensible course of action is to take the fine woman out for a nice meal when she gets home, give her a big bunch of flowers, then explain how tired he has been what with the long hours that those cheap bastards in the gallery were making him work. It's a good plan. But Lenny makes one small error of judgement. He stops off to see an old musician friend on his way home. One thing leads to another, Lenny doesn't get home, not for another twelve hours. It's now ten o'clock in the evening and Mrs Lenny has been waiting three hours for him to come through the door. When he finally arrives things just aren't quite the way he planned them. The flowers, a bunch of her favorite tulips purchased at considerable expense, don't have heads on them anymore. They were dead-headed in the subway doors when some dink nudged him. And his breath now reeks of bourbon and cigarettes. Also, it happens to be too late to go out for dinner, because she has to go to bed to get up early for her job, a job she hates but which has supported them, intermittently, when he wasn't employed. Lenny explains that these small lapses in judgement were all done with her best intentions at the forefront of his mind and heart. He didn't get a cab home because he didn't want to wake her. He stopped off at his friend's house because he needed to borrow some money to take her out to dinner. And he started drinking because his friend was so depressed about his life, he wanted someone to drink with.

His wife does not respond. Just looks at him. Lenny whips out his present.

'Tulips, baby,' he crows. 'Remember? They're your favorites!' Only they are not tulips, they are a bunch of stalks. And she's not that impressed.

The only thing she has to say, and this after a minute's reflection, is, 'Lenny, you know how Bill Clinton says this is the time for change?' And he says, 'Yeah, baby,' thinking she's going to change the habit of a lifetime and vote. But she doesn't. She tells him, 'I've been thinking about our marriage . . .' And as those words come tumbling off her lips, he feels his legs buckle, the bile rise in the back of his throat, and a terrible urge to vomit. He knows exactly what's coming next. It comes. She wants some space to think about their marriage, so why doesn't he move out for a while?

Thus in the space of just two days Lenny's life has completely disintegrated. No wife, no job, no home.

We were birds of a feather.

3

As all good Eagle Scouts know, any big trip into the woods requires extensive planning and preparation, and this one was no exception. We spent the next two mornings researching one of the most important purchases for this ride, the car stereo. Sitting six weeks in a car, you have to have a pumping stereo. We tested many in the stereo stores down on Canal. Most weren't loud enough. We settled on a Sony deck with a six-channel amp and a complementary-component speaker kit. It was costly, but when the man hooked it up and turned it on, it made the windows vibrate on the electrical store across the street and a man drop his lunch on the sidewalk.

For advice on final choice of route we drove uptown to visit the American Automobile Association. According to the *New York Times*, this venerable institution offers a useful service for the traveling motorist: the scenic route map. I wanted one of those. The offices are up on Broadway around 63rd Street. They have beautiful color posters on the walls with invitations like 'Visit Niagara!' And 'Come to the Keys!' It's a place to make the traveling motorist feel instantly at home.

At the counter I asked the lady for a map of Central and South America. She returned shortly with two maps in her hand, five dollars each. I asked her if it was true that the AAA would mark out a scenic route for a new member.

'Of course!' she replied. 'From where to where, sir?'

'New York City to the Copacabana Beach, Rio de Janeiro, Brazil,' I said. 'Please.'

'*Where?*'

'Brazil.'

She laughed, a thin-lipped type of laugh. 'Ha ha ha!'

I asked her what was so funny.

'We don't *do* scenic routes outside the US.'

'No?'

'United States only. Anyway, it's *impossible* to drive there at the moment.'

'Why's that?'

'Road's up at Guatemala City.'

'All of them?'

'There *is* only one.'

This contradicted the information on the map I had just been sold. But I didn't argue. This lady was stuck in New York City, about to face the worst winter in decades, possibly history if you were to believe the weathermen, and my partner and myself were on the brink of embarking on a long, leisurely ride through Central and South America, ending up at the great carnaval and perhaps one or two of the better Lambada Halls. Life is not always fair. The lady asked me what car I was taking. I pulled out the polaroid I had now taken to carrying about in my wallet. I slid it over the counter.

'Ha ha ha!' she said. 'What you really going in?'

I pointed at the polaroid.

'You guys want to drive all the way down to Brazil in a *hearse*?'

'Yes.'

'To see?'

'The carnaval.'

'The *carnival*.'

'No, carn*a*val. It has an "a".'

'Carn*a*val.'

'That's right. And maybe some Lambada Halls.'

She laughed. 'Well, if you want *my* opinion, gentlemen . . .'

Advice. You can never get enough when setting out into the unknown. That's my motto.

'What's your opinion?' I asked.

'You haven't got a snowflake's chance in hell of making it!'

'Why's that?'

'Some of the places you'll pass through don't *have* roads. Dirt tracks, mud slides, burst rivers, mule tracks – only a four-wheel could possibly *hope* to get through. Anyway, even if you *had* a four-wheel, what are you going to do when you get stuck? The AAA does *not* offer relay facilities outside the United States!'

I did not spend fifty-five good dollars to join the AAA. But I did learn something useful: you don't *need* car insurance to drive through South America – probably because nobody will give it to you anyway. Whatever the reasons, this was good. It would save money for more useful things like bribes and drinks.

Route research and car preparation were now finished. Took us about a day and a half. Next job was getting the right clothes.

To drive to Rio without being shot, arrested, robbed, raped, fed to the pigs or made into a Marxist revolutionary was not going to be easy if you are to believe half the stories you read in the papers. Civil war in parts of El Salvador and Guatemala. American sentiment running at an all-time low in places like Nicaragua, Panama, Colombia, and Bolivia, courtesy of American foreign policy and the DEA. The Shining Path, the Peruvian Marxist guerilla group, were out of their caves in the mountains and down on the coastal plains stopping and shooting passing traffic on the only road down to Lima from Ecuador. Pablo Escobar, the Colombian narco-gangster, had busted out of his three-bedroom suite at the local jail and was busy waging a non-discriminatory bombing campaign against all banks, hotels and other civil institutions in retaliation for the government's refusal to grant the fat fuck a pardon. Rebels had kidnapped missionaries in the Darien Gap and put a million-dollar price-tag on the head of each of them. All in all, it was not a great season for the average motor-tourist. But an undertaker? That was different. That was my theory.

Years ago I had seen on the television a short, bleak report from El Salvador or Nicaragua showing the burial of one of the country's most notorious mass-murderers. This man, I think he was a politician, had spent many good years murdering, torturing and incarcerating the local citizenry in the name of freedom and democracy. He died, as a lot of them seem to do, peacefully, in his sleep, surrounded by family and relatives. The reporter was watching the funeral from the sidewalk, I was in my LA-Z-BOY with a beer and cigarette waiting for a movie, and I wasn't watching this piece for more than thirty seconds when I realized something quite grotesque was taking place on those streets – *nothing*. No mob scenes. No lynching. None of that. Over the years this man must have touched and possibly ruined the lives of every man, woman, and child standing there, and yet . . . nothing was happening. The populace watched in reverent silence and the cortège crept down the street unmolested.

At the time I could draw only two conclusions from this: Latins must have a respect for the dead and the ritual of funerals which transcends the deepest and most heartfelt feelings of anger and revenge. Also – and this was a trivial conclusion, but one that was pertinent to what I was hoping to do – if you don't want to get your wang pulled in South America, get yourself a hearse. I now owned a hearse. It was time to *look* like I owned a hearse.

Essex Street on the Lower East Side of Manhattan is next to an old Jewish neighborhood where they sell great pickles, if you're a pickle lover. It was the only place I could think of to buy an undertaker's attire. I bought three Hasidic long coats from a second-hand clothing store. Then I went next door to a wedding outfitter's to buy top hats.

The shop assistant said, '*Your* wedding, sir?'

He was a cheery man. I pointed out the window at my hearse. He stopped smiling.

I bought three hats and three sets of white gloves. Preparations were now finished. I had been to see my doctor to get the right jabs and a prescription for malaria pills. I had called all the embassies, told them what I wanted to do and asked them if they had any tips for me. They usually only had one: 'Why don't you fly?'

My family were also a little worried about this trip.

'There are easier ways to kill yourself,' my grandmother told me, 'than driving to goddamn Brazil.'

Then she told me about a friend of hers up in New Hampshire, who knew a girl, who had a sister, who had a best friend, who was a cousin of a young girl, who had a father with this friend, who happened to be a maid for a nice family in the Chicago area, who were of the opinion that I would be lucky to get through Mexico in one piece, forget Brazil.

Everybody has friends with this opinion.

4

Midnight on Broome Street. Through the back door of the hearse we'd stacked a couple of cases of beer, two Central and South American guide-books, two road maps, a bin-liner of clothes, one skateboard, one set of woolly ear-muffs from K-Mart, one St Christopher, one Our Lady of the Highway charm, a Martini kit, a First-Aid kit, a vacu-packed kielbaasa sausage and finally the *Manual de Lambada* (beginner's guide). Anything else we might need – curtains, bibles, rosaries, religious icons – could and would be purchased on route.

As the final muted chimes of midnight rang out from the church on Mott Street, the glove compartment was opened, volume 1 of my friend Leonard Leonard's *Music To Drive To* was introduced, a number of little green lights started winking furiously on the deck as the power surged up on the amp hidden behind the seat, and a hiss erupted in the front parlor making two-and-a-half tons of chrome, leather and naugahyde shake as Deep Purple kicked in with 'Hey, Joe!' – my friend Leonard Leonard felt we had an obligation, as drivers of a funeral car, to carry some good soul music. Deep Purple was his idea of a good soul band.

The 'On Appointment' sign was fixed up in the front glass, the shifter was slid down into drive, I stomped on the big gas pedal and nine-and-a-half liters of V8 spat life into the rear whitewalls, churning up heaps of just-fallen snow, as the hearse leaped away from the curb, bucking, shuddering and snaking violently down that empty, dark street toward the West Side Highway and the long road south.

It was important, I felt, to start something like this in the way you meant to continue . . .

5

The ideal route from New York to the beach in Rio is to run south on the Jersey Turnpike, pick up 78, head east over to 81, then drop south through the Appalachians to Knoxville, take 75 and then 59 into New Orleans, the Funeral City and then just south for 10,000 miles. The way not to go is south till daylight, then put in some west when you can see the signs – which is what we ended up doing. New Orleans was our first scheduled port of call and it was an important one. Lenny had a useful friend in New Orleans, Mr Rick Chenier. Chenier was a genuine mortician; educated at one of the top undertakers' colleges in the United States, not a faker like us. Chenier had his own business. He was the man to talk to about undertakers' protocol, curtain choice, and other useful tips to ease our rapid route south. With application, with no

mechanical failure, with the 'On Appointment' anti-cop pro-
phylactic high and visible in the glass (troopers don't give
speeding tickets to hearses flying down the highway in the
middle of the night if they're working – another theory) we
planned on arriving in New Orleans shortly after midnight
the following day. If all went according to plan.

However, fifteen minutes out of New York City, after
watching the twinkling lights of the city recede in the rear-
view for the last time for who knew how long, the world
suddenly started to revolve.

'What are you doing?' Lenny asked.

'Nothing.'

'Well, *do* something, goddammit!'

We had started spinning in a slow loop and I had no idea
why. Opposite wheel-lock, powering up and not braking to
get some bite back on the big whitewalls – I tried all these
emergency counter-measures but they had absolutely no
effect on the course the old hearse took as it whupped down
the empty, snow-covered tarmac of the New Jersey Turnpike.
We made a perfect 180-degree turn over two empty lanes of
highway until friction finished this unwanted performance
and drew us up to a juddering halt, in a loose bank of fresh-
fallen snow, facing the wrong way.

Lenny wiped his drink off his holed sweater. 'What
happened?'

'No idea.'

'You know what I think? I say we trade this bitch in and
get a four-wheel.'

My partner had not fully adjusted to the idea of traveling
in a funeral car. The first time I took it out to Brooklyn to
pick him up, he said, 'D'you know what kind of car this is?'

'A Cadillac.'

'No,' he said, 'this is *not* a Cadillac. This is a fuckin' *hearse*. A car that carries *dead* people. There is a small difference.'

I explained things to him of course. But he was still not convinced that driving in one of these wasn't asking for trouble. Now here we were, fifteen minutes out of New York City, and he had his drink down his front. It was not the most auspicious start. I got out into the cold and walked around the vehicle. We had a flat. It took us about a half-hour to change. When it was fixed we stopped at the next truck stop to warm up, and buy olives.

One-thirty, in my experience, is a good time to visit a truck stop. Nobody's there. But there were some rigs parked in the truck lot adjoining the car park waiting for the weather to clear. We went inside.

'Hey!' a voice called out. 'You the guys that just pulled in here in that goddamn hearse?'

By the window facing the lot where the hearse was parked, there were two lines of vacuum-formed plastic tables. Halfway down sat a group of three truckers and one woman. At another table sat a solitary trucker. The man that just called to us had a lady draped around his shoulder. She wore a cheap red blouse that was cut low across her cleavage, a tight pair of stone-washed jeans, white Reeboks and that dye in her hair that when put on black hair turns it orange. They sat sipping coffee from a Thermos.

'That's us,' I said.

'Where you going, buddy – an appointment?'

The men thought this was a very good joke indeed.

'No,' I said. 'Brazil. Yourself?'

'*Brazil*? Holy shit! That's a *long* motherfucker of a drive. What the hell you boys going down to Brazil for?'

'Carnaval,' I said.

'And the Lambada!' said Lenny, clicking his fingers and making a dainty pirouette.

The solitary trucker, the one sitting away from the rest sporting a polished pair of 200-dollar ostrich-hide Tony Lama cowboy boots, wrangler Levis, a pressed polyester Big Man check shirt, crowned by a Winston Cup sportsman's cap, exhaled heavily and said, 'If you boys be going to Brah-zil, you be wanting to pass through Meh-heeko.'

'That's right,' I said. 'Mexico, Guatemala, El Salvador, Hon –'

'And if you goin' be goin' through Meh-heeko,' he interrupted, 'you won't be getting through there unless you drive *real* fast. Real fast, son.'

'Why's that?'

'First twenty-five miles over the border is Deadman's Land. Bandeetos.'

He managed to make this sound about as threatening as being attacked by a box of breakfast cereal, Cheerios, perhaps. Or maybe Wheaties.

'Place is full of 'em. Them sons of bitches will steal your rig before you can say "*hola, amigo*". It's goddamn *law*less.'

I was just about to ask him for a cup of coffee when he informed us that he had been down there. To bandit-infested Meh*eeko*.

'You *have*?' said a trucker.

'Uh-huh. One time a coupla years back I had to run a load down to Mex City. They had some big construction going on down at the embassy there. So I picked up in San Diego, ran down to Laredo, pulled in there early evening, but the goddamn border guards told me they wouldn't allow me to run to Mex City unaccompanied. Hell, I tol' them chilli beans where to git. But the *jefe*, he still wouldn't allow it. He sent an armed guard of six men with me, all the way to Mex City, in an old two-door Ford. Took me seventy-two hours of straight running to git there. Roads the worst I ever bin on, and man I been on plenty a bad ones' –

'I'll bet you have,' said another trucker. 'I'll bet you have.'

'Shit, in Mexico you come hauling round the mountain on a strip of dirt no wider than these two tables put together, and right there, man, *right* fuckin' there, will be some goddamn bus or truck wreck! Drivers all fucked up! The one I almost run through was waving a bottle of mescal, grinning at me like some goddamn *chim*panzee. I'm telling you, if that *jefe* hadn't insisted I ride with an escort, I probably wouldn't be here today . . .'

No great loss. I said, 'It sure is cold out there, isn't it?' casting a hungry eye on the man's Thermos of coffee.

'*Cold!*' he exclaimed. '*Cold!* This ain't cold. Hell, no! Why, I remember one time I was coming back from Canady and –'

'Lenny?' I said.

'*Yes?*'

'Let's go.'

'Any of you boys got any olives? . . . No? Never mind.'

Just before we left I asked the fearless trucker his name. I was hoping it might be something like Bandit or Outlaw.

'I ain't got no name,' the nugget told us.

6

My hearse worried me that first night out on the road. It weaved and wallowed and wouldn't track straight and that wasn't the Martinis. But by eleven the next morning I was feeling much happier. The heat was up, the highway was now clear of snow, the big V8 was thrumming along silent, vibration-free, probably most happy to be given the opportunity to strip the carbon from its coagulated pipes after twenty years of dawdling about in a city, but it was the view through the big glass windscreen that first morning in the hill country of Virginia that got the blood coursing through the veins, dispelled any insidious feelings of doubt caused by the handling troubles, and reassured my partner and myself that we had absolutely nothing to worry about with this twenty-year-old funeral car. The effect it had on other road-users was inspirational. Two flashes with the lights, a fist on the horn, and the car ahead would swerve out the fast lane, heads in the interior would then swivel, and there would be this look as we spat past, Lenny waving at everybody from behind his sunglasses, top hat and Martini glass. It was a fine morning out there on the road. Just the way things ought to be.

A little past the town of Pulaski I spied a hunched, frozen figure standing at the roadside. He was small and gaunt, in his forties, wearing a cheap red Sears wind-breaker, over-sized jeans, a large faded blue sport-fishing hat with a long bill and Chuck Taylor lo-tops. He looked miserable. His thumb was out. I hit the brakes.

'What are we doing?' Lenny asked.

'Picking up that hitcher.'

'Good idea.'

The man came running down the road until he realized what type of automobile had just pulled over on to the hard-shoulder to pick him up. Then he stopped and stared. Lenny threw open the door. Cautiously, the man approached.

'*Entra!*' said Lenny.

During the night we had listened to a *Teach Yourself Spanish!*

tape I had been given for Christmas. *Entrar* is Spanish for to enter. *Entra, entras, entra! Entramos, entráis, entran!* And so on.

The fellow wasn't familiar with it.

'Are you boys, ah, morticians?' he asked.

'Tourists,' I replied.

'Tourists?'

'Yeah.'

Seeing two men sitting in a large funeral car, both red-eyed from lack of sleep, unshaven, wearing top hats and long coats, sitting in a rubble of beer cans, hamburger wrappers and polystyrene cups, listening to loud beat music and claiming to be tourists not morticians seemed to confuse him. From the time he took deliberating whether he should get in the car with us and be warm, or stay outside and freeze to death, I'd say he didn't think there was an awful lot to it. But it was sub-zero outside, nobody else had stopped to pick him up, he wasn't wearing enough to keep a sparrow warm, so we knew and he knew he didn't have much choice in the matter. He slid in the front and soon we were back in the fast lane, cars jumping out of the way, the needle on the speedometer flickering up around the ninety mark, the man's eyes glued to it.

'So,' Lenny asked, lighting a cigarette, 'where you headed, friend?'

'Pensacola.'

Pensacola is on the Florida pan-handle. Lenny nodded. He pulled a bottle of bourbon from the mobile liquor store he liked to call an overcoat.

'Like a snort?'

'Is that a safe thing to do? Drink and drive?'

'*I'm* not driving. *He's* driving. I'm drinking. You want some?'

'No, thank you.'

'How about beer? You want beer? Got a coupla cans down here somewhere if you're interested. Let me see now . . .'

A sweeping search under the bench seat revealed a couple of hamburger wrappers, three empty cigarette packets, five or six empty amphetamine wraps, a twisted can of soda and finally a dented can of beer.

'There you go.'

'You like to drink in the morning, huh?' the man asked.

'On special occasions,' Lenny replied.

'What's the occasion?'

'I'm getting divorced.'

'I'm sorry to hear that.'

'So am I. Three years of my life down the tubes and what have I got to show for it?'

'Heartache?'

'Uh-huh.'

'Misery?'

'You got that right.'

'And alimony.'

'Sounds to me like you must have been through the Terrible Trinity yourself.'

'Two times,' said the man.

Cautiously, he turned to inspect the coffin compartment. 'This is a real hearse, huh?' he asked.

'A 'seventy-three,' I replied. 'A banner year for hearses, I'm told.'

'Jeez.'

'What's your name?' I asked him.

'Earl.'

'Earl, it's a pleasure to meet you,' I said.

'Where you guys going?'

'South.'

'Yeah. Me too.'

Earl started to rub his hands in the jet stream from the heater.

'Travel much, Earl?' Lenny asked.

'I'm in the merchant marine. I been some places.'

'Merchant marine, huh? How about that?'

'Yeah, I work on freighters out of Baton Rouge, Louisiana. I been over to Africa and I been down to Venezuela a coupla times, too.'

'That's very interesting, Earl. Very interesting. And you know what? Maybe, you're just the guy we've been looking for.'

'Huh?'

'To assist us.'

'I don't understand.'

'Earl, let me explain a few things here. We're going to be making a fast run down the Pacific coast of the Americas to cross the Andes in – where the hell we going across?'

'Arequipa,' I said. 'That's about one thousand kilometers south of Lima. Or maybe we'll drop down to Chile, then cut across Argentina.'

'There you go. Anyway, last night, Earl, last night we were driving, driving, driving. All through the goddamn night. Discussing all manner of important personal and highly confidential topics; being *vigilant*, you understand. And at some point, I don't recall exactly when, we started making some calculations.'

'What sorta calculations?' Earl asked.

'Fiscal ones, Earl. Fiscal ones.'

'Yeah?'

'That's right. Now, my friend here, he has a *lot* of money.

Don't ask me to tell you how *much* because it could be *incriminating*, you understand what I'm saying?'

'It's illegal money?'

'Doesn't matter if it is. But he's got a *lot*. That's the important thing. A *lot*.'

'Jeez, what you planning on *doing*?'

'Everything,' I said.

'And that costs money, Earl. Fun doesn't come cheap these days. But you travel in a vehicle like this and you develop fiscal problems. Hell, you got *assets*, am I right?'

'I don't understand.'

'This hearse, you can see for yourself, it's a working car. Fully operational. Twenty years of excellent service. Twice – am I right? – *twice* blessed by the Bishop of New York?'

'That's what Tony said.'

'Smooth, silent, comfortable, air-conditioned, luxury quality, but – and here's my question to you, Earl – what do *you* think the chances might be of picking up some freelance work on the way down?'

'Freelance work?'

'You know. Funerals, man.'

'*Funerals?*'

'Earl, listen to me. Have you ever buried anyone?'

'No.'

'Ever *wanted* to bury anyone?'

'No.'

Lenny shrugged. 'A car like this, think that is an option you might consider? If you run into fiscal problems?'

'Not really.'

'Let me ask you something then. How much would you pay *us* to bury *you*?'

'I beg your pardon?'

'You're what? Five ten? A hundred and sixty pounds? Shit, a hole like that'd take—'

'Long time,' I said.

'South America?' said Lenny. 'Got to be a land of opport*unity* for the travelling mortician. War, poverty, crime, disease, famine – it's all *there*, Earl. Did you know par examplar – that's Spanish, Earl – did you know that down in the city of Medellin – that's in Colombia; a place with perhaps one-*eighth* the population of New York City – in Medellin they got a yearly murder rate *eight* times higher than New York City?'

'I didn't know that.'

'Does that *tell* you something?'

'It sure does.'

'What's it tell you?'

'Just here'll be fine, thank you, boys.'

'What?'

'I said pull over right now and I'll be getting the hell out, you crazy bastards.'

I pulled over. Earl got out. Back on the highway we commiserated with the loss of our first hitcher, but the encounter gave us something to think about on the run through the states of Tennessee and Alabama: a company name. To make us legit. We decided on one: The Burial Brothers, the world's first traveling morticians . . .

7

Laffite's Blacksmith Bar in the French Quarter of New Orleans was our first destination when we arrived some twenty-four hours after departing New York City.

Just outside the city limits, coming over Lake Ponchartrain, we had met two car fans in an old Ford pick-up truck. They wanted to engage us in a friendly conversation about the performance characteristics of the 472 V8 in a '73 Cadillac hearse. Eighty miles an hour, in the fast lane, and this toothless bib'n'braces type is leaning out his window, yelling, 'NICE FUCKING RIDE, DUUUUUUDE!' It wouldn't have happened in any other motor-car. It was a warm and generous welcome to the city of New Orleans.

Laffite's has swing-doors, a brick bar, and sawdust on the floor. At the bar Lenny pulled me over to one side and jabbed a thumb over his shoulder at the young lady standing behind him pulling beer at the pumps. 'She,' he said, 'would look *great* in the hearse. Don't you think?'

The young lady wore a black top, black jeans, black hair, black eyeliner, black nail-paint – everything on her was black except for her teeth, her skin and her two eyes.

'She's very pretty,' I said.

'Watch. I got a line no girl could possibly refuse. Oh, miss?'

The girl came over. She had a nice smile. But she was worried. Having Lenny lean over the bar and grin at her like some predatory reptile made her feel uneasy.

'Can I help you gentlemen?' she asked.

'As a matter of fact,' said Lenny, 'you can. We'd like a *drink*.'

'What kinda drink, sir?'

'Well,' Lenny said, 'this is how it is, sweetheart. My partner here and myself have just driven all the way down from New York City in that ol' hearse parked outside. You like hearses, sweetheart?'

'I don't know.'

'They grow on you. Anyway, we drove *all* of last night, *all* of today, and now here we are in the great Laffite's Blacksmith Bar before closing. So what would you recommend to two weary road dogs as a sorta celebratory drink-and-pick-me-up kinda idea?'

'I don't know. Beer?'

'*Beer?*' Lenny snapped. 'Now, that doesn't sound very imaginative, does it?'

She shrugged.

'But if a pretty girl like you thinks beer is the *right* drink to have, we'll take a coupla beers,' he said. 'Bass?'

'Two Bass?'

'Two Bass.'

She took two tall glasses from the bar and poured.

'How am I doing?' Lenny asked.

'I think she likes you.'

'Watch this – say, miss?'

'Mm-hm?'

She poured off one mug, put it on the bar, and started the pump on the other.

'What are you doin' later?'

She smiled. 'Oh, I don't know. Nothin' much, I guess.'

She put the second beer up on the counter next to the first. Lenny leaned up on the bar and grinned. 'Would you like to come to Rio with us?'

'What?'

'I said, would you like to come with us to Rio de Janeiro, Brazil? They got this little carnaval starting up there in about six weeks. We're driving there in that ol' hearse parked outside, if you're interested.'

The girl looked at Lenny and then myself leaning up against her bar. She peered out through the swing-door at the dull sheen on the hearse parked at the curb. The car was a little dirty after 800 miles. But it was clearly a hearse and nothing else.

'You guys really going all the way to Rio in *that*?'

I nodded.

'Far out!'

'Isn't it?'

Lenny leaned a little closer over the bar. 'So how 'bout it? Wanna come?'

'Wow,' she said. 'I'd *love* to go to Rio with you guys. That'd be so cool.'

'Good. When d'you finish?'

'But it ain't that easy.'

'Sure it is.'

'Nuh-uh. I'd have to know your star signs before I could agree to go *anywhere* with you guys.'

'Star signs?' said Lenny. 'What fucking star signs?'

'You know, like in the zodiac?'

'Oh,' said Lenny, laughing. '*Star* signs. Of course. How *sen*sitive. I'm the red-blooded bull, baby. I'm Taurus.'

'How 'bout you, Billy Balou?' she asked me with a smile.

'Leo,' I said. 'The lion.'

'The lion and the bull,' the girl said, shaking her head sadly. 'That's a problem.'

'Why's that?' I asked.

'You're both fire signs.'

'So?'

'I'm a *water* sign.'

She waited to see what effect this had. It didn't.

'What normally happens with fire signs and water signs is one extinguishes the other,' the girl said. '*Pff!* Like that! That's why if I were to go, I don't think it would work.'

'Excuse me,' I said. 'Does offering to give you a ride from

here to Brazil sound like a two-alarm fire? No, it doesn't. With all due respect, what it sounds like to me is a once-in-a-blue-moon opportuni –'

'Wouldn't work,' she replied. 'Not in a zillion, trillion years.'

Lenny leaned further over the bar. 'Are you trying to tell me that you won't come down to Rio because it's written in the fucking *stars*?'

'I am.'

'What are you? Stupid?'

'Y'see?' she said. 'You see what I mean? There you go. Being a fire sign. In-credible. Here, look at this.' She bent over and pulled out the *Times-Picayune*, spread it open and turned to the E-section. On the page behind the funnies of Calvin and Hobbs, Cathy, Andy Capp, Peanuts, The Wizard of Id, and Doonesbury, and underneath the TV selection, were the horoscope columns.

She pointed her finger to the third column.

'Read,' she said to me.

I read: 'Leo. July twenty-three to August twenty-two. Running errands for a friend who's sick or swamped is an easy way to be a hero. Double-check figures and instructions before the final go, as errors are evading your eye today. Aries inspires and has what you need –'

'You see?' she said.

I didn't see anything at all. *Running errands for a friend who's sick or swamped is an easy way to be a hero? Aries inspires and has what I need?* What's that got to do with thumping down to Rio in a nine-and-a-half-liter hearse?

'No,' I said.

'Read this,' she said to Lenny, pointing him to Taurus. 'You'll understand.'

He read: 'Taurus. April twenty to May twenty. Don't be so

hesitant to let a lover know how attached you are. Others need affection as much as you do.'

He looked at the girl and squeezed her hand. She smiled. He said, 'You know something?'

'What?'

'I think you may have something there.'

'Yeah,' she replied. 'But not with you.'

We didn't stay in Laffite's for a second beer.

8

There was no paint in the halls of the third floor when I walked down it first thing next morning to bang on Lenny's door. We were in a motel downtown. The wallpaper was peeling away with damp, the numbers on his door were 3, then a space, then another 3, swinging upside-down. The door was one of those sheetrock jobs, caved in at the base, where somebody had tried to kick it in.

'Lenny?' I called.

There was no response. I banged again. Still no response. I shouted. Finally there was a snort of recognition, then a fierce rustling of the bedclothes, then the creak of old bed-springs, and ... a settled but deep drone of contented snoring.

'LENNNNNNNY!'

'WHAT?'

'Open the door.'

'Huh?'

'Open the door. I need to talk to you.'

A heavy pad of footsteps. Then the door swung open and there, loosely wrapped in the shroud of his bedding, looking like a rapacious carnivore after ripping apart half an elephant, was Lenny.

'Morning,' I said.

'Says who?'

'Let's have breakfast.'

'*Breakfast?*'

'Yes.'

'D'you know what *time* it is?'

'About seven.'

'Seven?'

'About that.'

'Why are you waking me at seven?'

'We have business to do.'

'What *business*? I'm on *holiday*, remember? I'm meant to be *recuperating*.'

I explained the day's itinerary: breakfast, mortician, car service, lunch. Lots to do.

'It can wait,' he said. 'I have to sleep.'

'You can sleep in the car,' I offered.

'And I can sleep in the *bed*, too. And I know which one I'd *prefer.*'

'I'll get coffee,' I said. 'You take a shower.'

It took me two hours to prize Lenny loose from that hotel room. He was fond of the place. It had been good to him. During the night he had started to paint again, something he hadn't done in a long time.

'How nice,' I said.

'Yeah. I can tell I'm going to get a *lotta* work done on this ride.'

When he was dressed he showed me the work. The talk had suggested a feverish three-hour stint of concentrated effort, but when he led me over to the cheap writing-table in the corner there was just one solitary A2 sketch on the desk underneath a pool of broken crayons, and empty beer cans.

'Here, check this out, man. Tell me what you think.' He lit a cigarette and opened a warm can of beer.

I inspected the work under the naked bulb hanging from the ceiling flex. It was a violently colorful and abstract idea, advanced well beyond my limited powers of interpretive analysis.

'Well?' he asked me.

'What is it?'

'Whatever you want it to be.'

'What's it worth?'

'Worth?'

'Money.'

'Who knows?'

'Let's sell it.'

'*Sell* it? I haven't even *started* it. This is just a *preliminary* sketch. It's a *long* process.'

'I thought it was finished,' I replied.

'No, no, no.'

I looked at the sketch again. It did seem a little rushed.

'This is three hours' work?'

'Not quite,' said Lenny, grinning. 'But a good twenty minutes.'

We ate breakfast in an old café with paint flaking off the walls down the street from the Mississippi. Lenny put in a call to Chenier to let him know we were coming. When he came back to the table he said, 'This is beautiful. I asked him about the curtains he used in his hearses and you know what he says? He only uses a deep burgundy velvet. Says it gives his hearses that Third Reich effect.'

Nazi hearse. Perfect. South America was full of dirty old Nazis.

Lenny persuaded the waitress to sit for him while I drank my coffee. His pencil brutalized the napkin with rapid, heavy movements. Last night had got him fired up.

'Let's go,' I said.

'Just like the good old days,' Lenny murmured, drawing away. 'Hey! That is *beau*tiful, baby.'

'Where you guys going?' the girl asked.

'To see an undertaker,' I said.

'We have to buy some curtains,' said Lenny.

'For our hearse,' I added.

'Oh yeah.' Her smile disappeared. '*That* hearse.'

Lenny held up his thumb, tilted it to one side, muttered something under his breath, nodded, spat on the paper, rubbed the mixture of saliva and lead into the paper in broad circular movements with his thumb and then snorted with approval. 'For you!' he said, thrusting the piece of paper in the young girl's face and giving her his best smile.

The girl studied it.

'That's *me*?' she asked.

Lenny nodded.

She smiled nervously. She plucked the drawing delicately from Lenny's hand as if it were a dirty diaper.

'That's great,' she said. 'Really.'

Rick Chenier lives in a quiet suburban street on the outskirts of New Orleans. It was like a hundred other suburban developments anywhere in the United States. Most of the ranch-style houses had station wagons, a garage, a small yard with some toys out on the front lawn. Pastel-colored curtains hung in new windows, new paint covered new weatherboards – it was a pleasant, friendly neighborhood development, a good place to raise kids. Rick's house was the one with the four hearses parked out front.

I pulled up. A tall thin man came bounding down the drive. He wore a T-shirt: *Grindhouse Graphics. Death Row Art & Collectibles*. He leaned through the window. Then he smiled. 'Nice to see you, Lenny.'

'A *great* pleasure to see you, too, Rick.'

'This yours?'

'Mine,' I said.

'Nice hearse, bud.'

'Thank you, Rick.'

'Am I right in thinking this is the 'seventy-three?'

'You are.'

'Always wanted the 'seventy-three. Is that with or without the cruise-control?'

'The last owner had cruise-control fitted.'

'Awesome.'

Fifteen minutes later we'd been introduced to Rick's beautiful wife and daughter and I was standing by the door of his office looking at an old wood and glass display cabinet. It had a sign on it. In festive green writing it said, 'Our Holiday Attraction!'

'That's a nice cabinet,' I said.

'Glad you like it.'

But then, getting up close, I noticed something.

'Is that an eyeball?'

'Yes, it is,' he said with a grin. 'I think there should be eleven. At least there was last time I counted.'

I counted ten. Some were blue, some green. They weren't the only curios he had in the 'Our Holiday Attraction!' cabinet. On the top shelf was a bottle of morphine sulfate, a bottle of Quaalude 300, a sign from the Undertakers Supply Co., some empty glass calibrated bottles marked Frigid Fluid, Chicago and a small wooden gravedigger statue, holding a spade in his right hand. On the plinth was written, 'Undertakers Need Love, Too'. On the second shelf were more glass fluid bottles and a graduating mug from a funeral school, with Rick Chenier's name printed above a picture of an old horse-drawn funeral carriage. Next to it were some paper advertisements for the Mack Haney and James M. Cole Funeral Home (Detroit's leading colored undertakers). On the bottom shelf was a pressurized steel container with gauges, part of an embalming kit. But this boded well. We had come to the right place and this excited me.

'Beautiful, huh?' said Rick. 'Now you wanna see some real cool stuff? Follow me.'

We stepped inside Rick's study. There was no writing desk in his study, no leather-framed photographs of the wife and daughter, no glass-fronted cabinets with loose stacks of papers, as you might expect to find in the study of a nice middle-class suburban dwelling. Instead, Rick's study was a mausoleum crammed with the three principal passions in his life beside the family. They were all connected with death. The first was a large collection of horror movie posters. Stacks of these posters were piled against his desk, mounted on boards, perhaps 200 of them, with titles like *Attack of the She Devils, Cry Baby Killer, They Came From Outer Space*, and so on. Then there was death camp memorabilia: concentration camp crockery, Nazi uniforms and framed correspondences from officers and victims of the Nazi camps. These were arranged on wall shelves and coat hooks around the room — which explained Rick's favored choice of curtain. Then there were certificates of execution from the states of Louisiana,

Texas and Florida sitting next to glass soil sample jars filled with earth taken from the gravesites of executed serial killers. But it was the last items to catch our attention that were the most revealing: framed color photographs of Rick with his arm around different men in prison overalls. Rick was grinning at the camera, proud as a rooster, as if he was standing next to his high-school football hero.

'Are they who I think they are?' I asked him.

'Who do you think they are?'

'Is that John Wayne Gacy, serial killer?'

'Yes, it is.'

'And is that David Berkowitz?'

'I'm their art dealer. Gacy sent my daughter a Christmas card. You wanna see it?'

'Rick, you are a sick, sick man,' said Lenny.

Rick grinned. 'I got one more thing you guys are gonna love. Follow me.'

We followed Rick down the hall to his daughter's room. He pointed at the corner.

'Ain't that just one of the most *beau*tiful things you *ever* saw?'

Standing against the wall, underneath a poster for Aerosmith, next to a small bed with a couple of teddy bears on the pillow, was a child's coffin, made of teak.

A little while later, sitting in the living-room listening to Rick's favorite artist, Doctor Feelgood, we were talking about the trip and the problems we might encounter down the road when I was suddenly struck with a simple solution to something that had been niggling away in my head since the day we left. In Peru fill-ups were going to be about as regular as a good meal. If we wanted to be sure we didn't run out of gas, we would have to carry gas containers. Gas containers always leak gas fumes. A hearse has no trunk. There is no place to isolate these cans and their fumes unless you put them outside the vehicle, either on the rear doors or the roof. But strapping a couple of cans to the outside would, I felt, compromise our identity. People would take one look at us and think, *Turista!* Not, *Funerario!* The solution — and I don't know why we hadn't thought of it before — was to *hide* the cans in something, then strap that something to the roof.

'You want a *coffin?*' Rick asked.

'That's what I'm thinking.'

'So you can put the gas cans *inside* this coffin.'

'Yes.'

'And then put the coffin *on the roof?*'

'Yes!'

'And that way people will just think —'

'We're having a busy day.'

'That's *beautiful!* I *like* that!'

'How much do coffins go for these days?' I asked.

'Depends what you need.'

'Something that won't rot.'

'Mine comes with a lifetime guarantee.'

'A couple of months should do it.'

'You know what?' said Mrs Chenier, smiling. 'I think we got something that might interest you. Hon? 'Member that little thing you were making in the garage?'

'What th— oh, *yeah*. That would be *per*fect, wouldn't it?'

Mrs Chenier smiled.

Rick said, 'I think this might be your lucky day, gentlemen.'

We followed Rick through the kitchen to the garage. Rick has a two-car garage. On the work-bench against the far wall, next to the lawn equipment and a Bass boat under a tarp on a trailer, was the item in question.

'I was gonna make a soap-box racer out of it for my daughter,' he sighed. 'But hey – if you guys want it, it's yours.'

It was a three-quarter size coffin. Made of pine.

9

One-thirty the following morning, shoveling hard across Louisiana State's I10 highway, heading non-stop for the Texas border after a successful day of shopping in New Orleans (bible, rosary, and music from Tower Records) we had a mechanical failure: a tonal change in the big V8's 1-5-2-6-3-7-4-8 firing pattern. Instead of that soothing, most comforting rumble that had filled our ears for mile after steady mile out there on the dark empty highway, faintly detectable under the blanket of loud music and the slurp of shrimp po'boys and vodka Martinis, the 472 suddenly revved – as if the shifter had been dropped from drive into neutral – the speed fell off, and we started to freewheel. But it only happened for a mere micro-second, then something caught, the rumble settled in, and the old hearse pulled down the flat empty highway under the dark quarter-moon sky as if nothing had happened at all. But it was enough to get the old alarm bells ringing.

'Lenny?'

He was busy fishing out a piece of shrimp that had fallen on the floor somewhere.

'*What?*'

'Did you feel that?'

'Feel *what*, man?'

'Something with the transmission.'

'I didn't feel nothing.'

'Transmission slipped.'

'You're imagining things,' he said. 'Go back to sleep.'

It happened again.

'Told you.'

'Goddammit, this car was only *serviced* five hours ago.'

'I know.'

'By a guy I *told* you not to use.'

'There was nothing wrong with Enrique.'

'Nothing a bottle of Geritol, a Spanish dictionary and some glasses couldn't fix. If I was to make one educated guess *why* we might be having this little problem with the transmission, I'd have to say it's because the man who *serviced* this automobile was handicapped.'

'Enrique wasn't handicapped.'

'Anybody who has to work listening to you babbling away in pidgin Spanish for a couple of hours is severely handicapped. To my mind.'

'Enrique told me he had twenty years of customer satisfaction in the automot—'

'That's not what he said.'

'Yes, it is.'

'No, it's not.'

'Okay. All right. What did he say?'

'He said he could fix it in twenty minutes.'

'He said that?'

'*Veinte minutos*, buddy. Not *veinte años*.'

We broke down a few minutes later.

Peering under the hood with a flashlight, I unscrewed the transmission fluid. The plastic dipstick was bone-dry.

'There you go,' I said. 'Thing has run out of fluid.'

'So we got a leak. Or we got a broke transmission. Either way, we're stuck deep in redneck territory and I'm half-Hebrew. This is not good.'

'I'll call a tow-truck.'

'Oh. That's an interesting idea. How? I don't see a town. I don't see a phone. In fact, I haven't seen a phone in thirty miles! And I don't see any cars. But of course it is two in the morning when any other sensible bastard is asleep in his bed, like we should be. But go ahead. Show me I'm wrong because I'm watchin'.'

A top hat, a beach shirt and a Hasidic long coat will attract a fair amount of attention from passing truckers. Within fifteen minutes the Louisiana State Highway Patrol had stopped to question us. Within thirty we were sitting in the warm cab of a tow-truck being pulled into the small backwater town of Vinton, by an old meth-head who hadn't been to bed in two days.

'Where you boys want me to put you down? I can take you to the garage. Or I can take you to the motel in town.'

'Motel will be fine,' said Lenny.

The man started chuckling and grinding his teeth.

'What's so funny?'

'You seen that movie, *Psycho*?'

'Sure. Long time ago.'

'You 'member what they call the hotel?'

'The Bates Motel.'

'The Bates Motel. Uh-huh. That's what we call ours, too.'

'Just put us outside the garage,' Lenny said.

Vinton was shut. It had a railroad running next to the main road. Just before pulling into the garage, the man said, 'Got a question for you, boys.'

'What?'

'Is it hard to get 'em to spread 'em in the back of that thing?'

'Spread what?'

'You know. Their *legs*.'

I paid him and he tore off into the night. The garage was opposite a Seven–Eleven. We went over. A middle-aged auto-mechanic leaned against the counter talking to the cashier, his sweetheart. I had a word with him. I described how my hearse had expired on me, ten miles out of town, and asked what he thought the trouble might be.

'Transmission's shot,' he replied.

'That's what I thought.'

10

'What you wanna know first?' the mechanic asked me. 'The good news? Or the bad?'

It was eleven the next morning. They had been working on the car three hours.

'The good,' I replied.

'Your transmission ain't shot. You blew a rear transmission seal. One of them'll cost you, oh, maybe six bucks to replace.'

'That's *beau*tiful!' I said, feeling a great wave of relief. 'So what's the bad?'

'Be about three hundred and forty dollars in labor.'

'Three hundred and forty dollars!'

'Plus tax.'

We were back on the road by five that night with a new front and rear transmission seal. The mechanic didn't think we'd have any more trouble with the seals or the transmission but he couldn't be sure.

'See, the transmission on the 'seventy-three General Motors Cadillac,' he told me, 'is a piece of shit. If it had been me, I'd have bought me the 'seventy-six. Transmission on the 'seventy-six is –'

'Yeah, but the 'seventy-three was the only one for sale.'

'I still would have bought me the 'seventy-six.'

This gave me something to think about as we bolted across Louisiana on to the Texas plains in the late afternoon and early evening. Transmission failure. Can't be many places south of the border that do transmission work on an old Caddy.

Around eight that night we stopped outside of Dallas for dinner at a place called the Hickory Grill (our beef is so fresh what you eat on your plate today was grazing grass yesterday!). For the rest of that night we rotated behind the wheel every two hours. During my shift I learned from the tape that 'Ayudame! Me estan robando!' translates as 'Help! I'm being robbed!'

II

The man at the speed shop, James Automotive on 803 San Dario, had seen our types before.

'So lemme get this straight,' he said as we stood at the counter, nine o'clock the following morning. 'You guys wanna jack that *hearse* about *ten* inches at the rear and a *couple* at the front?'

'Be nice,' I said.

'And you want to purchase a *super*charger?'

'Perhaps.'

'And if we don't have no supercharger, you wanna buy a *nitrous* kit?'

At some point on the ride down Lenny had shrewdly observed that if you were to have a supercharger under the hood, you could run at about 160 all day long. This can give a man great peace of mind when penetrating the more turbulent territories we hoped to pass through. Peace of mind is something you can never put too high a price on.

'And we want a socket set, a Cadillac workshop manual, a can of E-Z Start, a case of octane-booster, a car-buffer's kit, and one of those purple glow-rider strips that you fit to the underside of the machine to give you the Green Hornet look,' I said.

He smiled. He understood.

'Well, to be perfectly honest with you boys, I've supercharged Chevys, Pontiacs, Fords, a few Volkswagens even, but I never supercharged a *hearse*. However, I'd surely appreciate the opportunity to *try*. When do you need it done by?'

'This afternoon?'

The soonest he could get it done was two weeks. This was not satisfactory. Tarris Hill was irate, waiting for us down in Mexico City and Tarris is not a man to keep waiting.

'How 'bout a nitro kit?' Lenny asked, lighting a Marlboro. 'How much and how long to fit one of those alligators under the hood?'

A nitro kit would take a while to set up and install, too. Next item discussed was a suspension kit. We'd run aground on a railway crossing coming out of Vinton. The hearse needed lifting. We had discussed this. Lenny's view was simple; jack it four feet, like Big Foot, the monster truck. This was not in keeping with the disguise. It lacked the vital element of credibility. I explained this to the shop owner. He reached below the counter and pulled out a vacu-wrapped package.

'How 'bout this?' he asked.

He slid it across the counter: four tempered steel bars, flat, about a quarter of an inch thick, twelve inches in length, drilled with different holes. It was a standard lift-kit. The bars were to be inserted between the leaf springs and the rear axle; the ride height could then be elected by choice of hole. Four holes at four, six, eight, and a maximum of ten inches. Ten inches would be —

'Whad'ya think?' he asked.

I thought bars like these would snap coming off a hump-back bridge at high speed and I told him so.

He said, 'Well, they might. If you put it like that.'

'You have anything, you know, more durable?'

Calling around town, he located some custom limousine air-shocks (200 p.s.i. max) which would fit the commercial chassis of a '73 Cadillac. At full pump this would give between four and six inches of height at the rear — not ideal but better than dragging the pipes all the way down the Andes. Two hundred dollars. Man came round with the shocks soon after. For the front we bought a coil-spacer kit; a couple of lumps of rubber you insert in the front springs, lifting it a couple of inches.

We paid, loaded the boxes, then drove up the street to Felipe's. Felipe has a little business on the main drag in Laredo which we'd seen on the way into town. In the front is a shop which sells carpets, vertical blinds, awnings and floor-ing. But behind, in a narrow side street, there is a dirt yard with a wood shack and corrugated roof, a goat, a couple of loose chickens and three young Mexicans in jeans, boots, blue work-shirts and big hats who gave the hearse a three-window double-black tint job for seventy-five dollars plus tax. We didn't have time to find curtain material and get it cut and hung. With the windows tinted we drove down the street to Gonzalez Auto Parts. I told the man what we were doing. He said, 'Got it goin' on in a car like that.' Three hundred and thirty-nine dollars later we'd bought a puncture seal kit, two spare fuel-filters, two air-filters, two oil-filters, PC valves, two complete sets of spark plugs, two transmission-filters, one eight-ton bottle of Jac; two spare sets of indicator bulbs, two spare fan belts; a twenty-four-inch tire iron, a ten-in-one fuel funnel, a couple of quarts of Slick 50 transmission fluid, a case of all-season motor oil, two five-gallon plastic spare fuel containers, a black plastic console to put over the transmission hump which had a compartment for change, a place for cassettes and two circular can-sized holes for refreshments; a spare set of windshield wipers, a fifteen-foot tow strap, and a case of Gas Plus fuel additive.

In the afternoon we went to the salvage yard on the outskirts of town to trade the two rims Tony had left for two rims with tires. The man wheeled them out. They were taken from an old Sedan de Ville. He put them behind the bench-seat in the front, either side of the big amp that was bolted to the partition wall. I paid him fifteen dollars and we went down to the Royal Treat Car Wash, next to Julep's restaurant, open twenty-four hours. We had the hearse cleaned, polished and enfragranced (choice of seven: Lenny chose musk). Our last stop was the Luis Rodriguez Auto Center to book the car in for a final alignment check and lift-kit fitting. Lenny went off to make some calls to Brooklyn to see how things were at home, I met the chief of the shop, a man by the name of Oscar. Oscar took one look at the car, scratched his head and said, 'Is that what I think it is?'

'It's a hearse.'

'You got any stiffs in the back?'

'No.'

'I ain't working on *that* car if it got a *stiff* in the back.'

'No stiffs,' I said.

He walked over, cupped his hand to the side of his head and peered through the newly tinted double-black side window.

'So what the fuck is *that*?'

I looked through the window.

'That's a coffin.'

'No shit, Sherlock.'

I opened the side door. I lifted the lid. I pulled out one of the empty gas containers and showed it.

'For the spare gas.'

I told him what needed doing. He said it would take a couple of hours. That would take the time up to about six o'clock in the p.m.

'What time does the border close?' I asked.

'It don't. It's open twenty-four hours a day.'

I went to find a gun shop. I have a friend in Los Angeles who does a lot of business in South America. When I told him I was driving to Brazil to see the carnaval he said I'd better be packing.

'Only one weapon's worth taking down there,' he said. 'And that's a Tec-9. Good kill rate. Semi-automatic. Made of plastic. It's the ideal holiday gun. No metal detector's gonna detect shit when you walk that through customs. Only problem is the price. I'd have to charge you a thousand.'

I asked if he had anything cheaper. He offered me grenades.

'Some guy try hold you up? Throw a couple of these out

the window and *boom!* Motherfucker'll turn into *burrito*. I got two by the bed if you want 'em.'

'How much?'

'Two hundred a pop.'

Two hundred was reasonable. The only problem was getting them. My friend lives in Los Angeles. I live in New York. Fed-Ex or DHS do not transport unlicenced live munitions across state lines, especially when it's high explosives. In the end I figured I'd buy what I needed here in Texas. In Texas you'd think you'd have no problem buying powerful handguns. I did. The man wouldn't sell me anything without a license. In the end I bought three canisters of Mace.

At seven that night we were down at the bridge over the Rio Grande and the traffic was heavy. I showed the guard our passports, the title of the vehicle, the bill of sale, my international driver license – all the documents you need to drive through Latin America. I kept them all, with the money, the road maps, the loose bundles of different currencies, in my tool-box purchased from Bud's (You Buy More For Less). A strongbox fitted to the interior would have been better, but we didn't have the time to get one built, so I decided to carry everything on me wherever we went in my Tuff'N'Uff tool-box.

The border guard waved us through. We drove over the bridge. We were now in Mexico. An official in a blue uniform pointed us into a dust lot. I drove in, we parked in the sun and walked inside a crumbling honey-colored concrete building: Mexican immigration. The young lady behind the desk said something about having to clear the car with the *aduana*. The *aduana* was customs. They were over on the Calle de Lara. But they shut at five.

It was the first of many delays.

12

It was a fourteen-hour run from the border to the Hotel Londres in Mexico City, where Tarris was waiting for us. We were now about a week late. But we had enjoyed ourselves thoroughly in Laredo, courtesy of another friend of Lenny's, a local newspaperman, James Krane. Krane took us to all the colorful spots on the border.

As soon as I pulled up at the curb, a short, hunched little man came shooting out to investigate. He had thin, wispy gray hair and deeply etched lines on a nut-brown face. He took one look at us, crossed himself, and then scuttled back inside.

'You fetch Tarris,' Lenny said. 'I'll wait here. Let you guys have a minute to yourselves. How long has it been since you last saw each other?'

'A couple of years.'

'Be nice for you fellas to catch up.'

I walked down the path to the hotel. I had my hat, my white gloves, the hat I'd bought for Tarris and his gloves. The old man was sitting behind the counter when I walked inside.

'Señor Hill, por favor,' I said.

'El Inglés?'

'Sí.'

'Creo que el Inglés no es muerto.'

I told him I hoped the Englishman wasn't dead because I'd come to pick the bastard up. He looked at my dusty top hat. Then at the one I was carrying in my hand.

'Funerario?'

'Turista.'

He clucked and shook his head sadly. Then I heard the familiar grizzly tones of my old pal.

'Where have you been, bastard?'

I turned round.

'It's a long story.'

'I'll give you a long story.'

'No, just give me a hug instead.'

'Fuck off.'

I held out his gift. 'This is for you.'

'I could kill you,' he muttered. 'I could bloody kill you.'

'I bought you a large. It might be a little on the big side. But try it on. Go on . . . There! Like it? Now follow me. I got something I have to show you.'

I headed for the door. Tarris fell in behind, cursing me. I have never seen the old goat look so angry. But he was just as I remembered him. Piercing blue eyes. Broad build. Rough, chiseled face. One or two more scars on it.

Lenny was sitting on the hearse with his boots crossed, wearing his top hat and his old sunglasses, smoking, when we walked up.

'That,' I said, 'is Lenny. And that car there' – I pointed to the beast car, a little dusty after the run through the mountains and the plains – 'that's our ride.'

I put my hat on and lit a cigarette. Tarris looked at me. Then over at Lenny. Finally he looked long and hard at the hearse. I hadn't told him what I'd bought. After a minute he nodded his head.

'Reckless,' he pronounced.

13

So there were three of us now. Like the old Musketeers. To celebrate this final addition we decided to hit a few places in town. Having spent five days waiting for us to pick him up, Tarris had explored the nightlife. The first bar he proposed was in the Zona Rosa. We drew up outside and the bouncer started laughing . . . until I tossed him the keys and told him to park it.

Inside – it was called something like the Pussycat Lounge – the place was half-empty. Parquet dance-floor. Stage with piano. Revolving glass-mirrored ball. Long line of girls in short dresses standing at the bar.

'Excellent choice,' said Lenny. 'I *like* it.'

The hostess came over. We ordered three cuba libres. When the drinks arrived Tarris said, 'Señorita, prendes los, ehm, traveler's chequetas por la cuenta?'

'Claro, hombre!'

He pulled out a folder of checks from his jeans.

'Passaporte?' she asked.

'Ehm, no. How 'bout a nice licencia Australian?'

'*No!*'

'Bugger.'

I paid.

The hostess walked off.

'Forgot your passport?' I asked.

Tarris pulled out a handful of British passports.

'Which one?' he grinned.

'What are you doing with four passports?' Lenny asked.

'I always travel with a good supply. Can get you out of all sorts of tight spots. But the problem is, I don't want to *use* 'em.'

'I don't understand.'

'It's a little complicated.'

'What's he talking about?' Lenny asked me.

'I don't know,' I said. 'Tarris?'

'Yeah?'

'Explain yourself.'

'My checks.'

'What about your checks?'

'Not valid.'

'So what are they? Stolen?'

A crooked grin.

'Who are they stolen from, Tarris?'

'My*self*.'

'You stole your own cheques?' Lenny asked. 'That's unusual.'

Tarris struck a match and lit a roll-up.

'There is this large financial institution in England that has caused me a great deal of embarrassment over the last six months. These traveler's checks are my revenge.'

'We're traveling with a goddamn criminal,' said Lenny. 'Good.'

Tarris crossed his legs, put his pack of Rizla rolling papers in his tin of Old Virginia tobacco, and pointed at a young lady sitting at the bar.

'She is a beautiful young maid, wouldn't you say, fellas?'

'The girl chewing the gum?' Lenny asked.

'On the left,' said Tarris.

'You mean the one with the *orange* hair?' said Lenny.

'Her.'

'What are you going to *do* about it?'

Tarris grinned.

'O seño*rita?*'

The young beauty did not respond. She sat on her stool, chewed her gum, and stared up at the revolving mirrored ball above her.

He tried again.

Still no interest.

Tarris got up, went over and had a word in the young lady's ear. He pointed to our table. She shrugged and shook her head. The bartender put down the glass he was drying and spoke to the young lady. She exhaled heavily, got up off her stool, straightened her skirt, then followed Tarris back to our table. She had red shoes with little bows on their toes.

Tarris pulled out a chair.

The girl sighed deeply.

'Hables inglés, señorita?'

Another big sigh.

'I see. A bad night, eh? What's your name?'

'Ea?'

'Como te llamas, señorita?'

'Sandra.'

'*Sandra?* Now that's a pretty name.'

Sandra started humming.

'Like the music, Sandra?'

'Qué?'

'Te gusta la música?'

The girl nodded and smiled.

'You wanna dance?'

'Qué?'

Tarris held out his hand.

'Quieres bailar, Sandra?'

Sandra shook her head. She clicked her fingers in time to the beat, chewed her gum, but she didn't want a dance.

'Five bucks he doesn't get anywhere,' said Lenny.

'You don't have five bucks,' I told him.

'Lend me the five and I'll pay you back in Oaxaca.'

I took five dollars out of my pocket and gave it to him.

Tarris set to work. He began with an intense study of her palm, tilting it one way, then another. It caught Sandra's attention. She stopped humming and chewing and jigging up and down, and asked him what the hell he was doing.

'Looking at the futura,' he told her.

She asked him what he saw, in the *futuro*.

A great deal, apparently.

'Two children?' he asked.

'Qué?'

'Tienes dos niñas?'

Sandra's eyes widened.

'Sí!' she exclaimed. 'Tengo dos niños, sí!'

He pointed at the edge of her hand. This area determines the number of children a woman has at any particular time in her life. Sandra was impressed by this. I could see exactly what she was thinking: if this rough-looking bastard can get this right, what else can he see? A nice *finca* in the country somewhere? All the money in the national *lotería*?

Tarris flattened her hand on his knee, held it up to the light, tilted it one way, then another, and finally he frowned.

'Qué pasa, hombre?' she asked.

Tarris shook his head solemnly. 'I see you've had a very hard life, señorita.'

'Haven't they all?'

'Una vida muy durro, Sandra. Una vida muy, muy durro.'

'Verdad!' said Sandra. 'Tengo una vida de puta madre, hombre! Una vida de puta madre!'

Puta madre translates as the mother of a whore. Colloquially it is used with the same gusto as goddamn.

Tarris leaned closer. He rubbed his index finger back and forth over her palm.

'But, aquí, darlin'. I see, ehm . . . hope.'

He pointed at an area somewhere in the middle of her palm.

'Qué?'

'You sera contento, Sandra.'

'Sí?' She laughed.

'Sí.'

'Cuando?'

And just when young Sandra had decided that this old Cornish blagger was an oracle to be listened to, not ignored, a rancher sitting nearby with snake's eyes, a straw hat, a mustache, and a white short-sleeved polyester shirt tossed a cigarette at our table which hit Sandra on her left breast. She ignored him. The cigarette rolled across the table, then on to the floor.

'Continua, señor,' she pleaded. And then, putting her hand on his forearm and looking him in the eye, 'Por favor.'

Tarris edged a little closer.

'I see a rich man, Sandra,' he said. 'I cannot see *who* he is, but he has mucho dinero. And when you meet this man . . .'

Another cigarette came winging over to our table.

'You will have niños with him.'

Sandra sighed deeply. What *puta madre* news! She put her arm around Tarris's broad shoulders. She nuzzled his grizzly ear and then stroked the long scar at the side of his neck.

'Es tu, señor gringo?' she whispered.

The old crook smiled.

'Bailar, Sandra?'

'*Sí!*'

And that's all it took. The music swung into a big, brassy salsa, and Tarris led the young lady on to the floor. Then he showed us a dazzling, athletic display of pelvic dancing that had young Sandra breathless and in fits of raucous laughter.

Palmistry. This was something we would clearly need to master. Girls love it.

14

Eleven-thirty that night I had a strange and disturbing experience. By design and choice I had managed with great success to avoid almost any binding responsibility in my life. I had no wife, no kids, no career, a bank account only a year or two earlier, but standing under a street lamp in Mexico City outside the Hotel Londres waiting for Tarris to pack his bags, I felt it: Responsibility. It sat heavily on my shoulders and I felt the need to share it.

'Lenny?'

'*What?*'

'Why don't we stay the night here and leave tomorrow?'

'Why the hell would we wanna do something stupid like *that?*'

'Well, we're drunk.'

'So what? We're always drunk.'

'Mexicans are bad enough driving when they are sober. At this time on a Friday night they too will be drunk. The road to Oaxaca is up through the mountains . . . Don't you think it might be better if we left in the morning?'

'Why would we want to do something stupid like that?'

'You have a sail boat down in North Carolina. You love this boat. I love this car. Would you take this boat of yours out on the ocean, in the *middle* of the night, if you'd been drinking heavily *all night long?*'

'Listen,' said Lenny. 'I *always* sail my boat when I've been drinking all night long. You're not thinking straight any more, idiot. Get in the back. Lie down. Leave the driving up to me. I'm a fuckin' expert.'

An expert. I liked that idea. I opened the side door, crawled in the back and sprawled out on the futon. The last thing I remember hearing before falling into deep sleep was the squeal of tires and a wild cacophony of horns as the hearse lurched into a violent four-wheel drift while Lenny screamed at Tarris, 'Did you say *left?* If you mean fucking *left*, goddammit, tell me left *before* we get to the turn – not when we're *half* way *through* it! You got that? Before the turn, ass-hole! Now get us out of here. And get us out of here first time! *First fucking time man!*'

And I thought: my good friend, Lenny. Giving some back to Tarris on my behalf (Tarris had not yet forgiven me for arriving a week late to pick him up and had made many pathetic references to it throughout the night). The car is in safe hands.

15

The hearse was motionless. But it was upright. It wasn't resting in a ditch. Or on its side. Or on its back. All of which was positive, of course. It was six-thirty in the morning, the sun was just coming up, and I had woken peacefully after seven hours' uninterrupted sleep. The boys had done very well.

I slid open the glass partition separating the driving

quarters from the sleeping quarters. Tarris was leaning halfway out of the passenger window, sucking on a toothpick. He was watching something over by a tall cactus tree.

'Morning,' I said.

'Not for some.'

The figure in the undergrowth grunted. It was Lenny.

'What's wrong with him?'

'Sounds like the –'

The morning air suddenly exploded with the sound of heavy artillery fire.

'Stopped at this little lean-to on the side of the road, a while back. Mexican truck-stop. Interesting place, bunje. Had some jugo de naranja – orange juice. They give it you in a plastic bag, you know, with a straw and an egg. Had the bugger with an empanada. Seems to have upset his guts.'

'I'm happy to see you gentlemen made it through the night without any incidents.'

Tarris looked at me. Then he started giggling. It was about that time that I noticed my long coat. It was bunched up on the dash. It had burn marks in the back.

'Where did that come from?' I asked.

'What?'

'That hole in my coat.'

'Ah. Well that must have been from the, ehm, fire . . .'

'What fucking fire?'

'Only a little fire, bunje. Nothing to worry about.'

And then it all came out. The two of them, racing around Mexico City's Periférico, drunk as swine, trying to find the airport exit to go change bad traveler's checks. Two hours later they are still racing around the Periférico and nothing much has changed, except they've had a lot more to drink. Eventually the boys hire a cab to *take* them to the airport.

The cab leads them out to the airport perimeter road, and when the terminal finally comes into view, Lenny stomps on the gas and speeds past the slowing cab but fails to see the sleeping policeman (*topés* in Spanish). At about seventy, they collide with this two-foot-high concrete molehill and take off. The car lands heavily, bouncing all over the road and shorting the battery cables. Flames shoot out from the side of the bonnet. Lenny hits the brakes, the hearse comes to a ragged halt next to a rank of startled Mexican taxi-drivers. The two drunks leap out the car. They pop the hood, but they can't find the fire-extinguisher. Tarris grabs the first item to come to hand – my coat. The flames are smothered. The cables are now badly seared. Tarris makes some hasty running repairs with black electrical tape and soon all is fixed. But they still can't change money. The change shop wants to see a passport.

'So everything's back to normal?' I asked.

'Normal, present, and correct, bunje,' said Tarris with a big grin.

'So why,' I asked seeing that the ignition light was on and the shift lever was in drive, 'is the engine not working?'

'Ah. That's because we ran out of petrol.'

Drunk driving was banned forthwith.

'How you feeling, Len?' Tarris asked.

'I told you, man. I'm feeling pretty goddamn sick, if you want to know the truth.'

'But what are the symptoms?'

'Why do you wanna know.'

'Because I might be able to help.'

'Well, I got diarrhoea from that shit we ate at the truck-stop.'

'Is that *violent* diarrhoea, Len?'

'It ain't peaceful.'

'I got something for that. What else?'

'Well, my stomach feels like I got the Mexican army having artillery practice down there.'

'D'you have a fever, Len?'

'I don't know. I don't have a thermometer. But I'm hot, I know that much. I'm hot as a sonofabitch.'

The air-conditioning had also broken during the night.

'I'll sort that out later,' said Tarris. 'How about your head? D'you have a headache?'

'Yeah, but that could be my hangover.'

'Anything else?'

'No, I think that about covers it.'

'Back in a jiffy.'

Tarris wriggled through the sliding glass partition into the back. In the rear-view I saw him rootling around in his canvas holdall. He emerged holding a dirty plastic wash-bag with a tropical scene printed on it. He unzipped the bag. It was packed to the brim with vials, creams, tubes and ointments.

'What you need,' said Tarris, holding up a pill-box, 'is one of these little men.'

'What's that?'

'From an old merchant seaman friend of mine,' said Tarris. 'Lives in a chapel near me at Trevillet.'

Tarris held out a small plastic container. Lenny took it and studied the label.

'Tetracyclin,' he read.

'A miracle drug. Can cure you of just about anything.'

'*Man*,' said Lenny, peering into the open mouth of Tarris's wash-bag. 'You got more pills in there than a goddamn pharmacy, Tarris.'

'It's important to travel with a useful selection of pharmaceuticals, Lenny. You never know what you're going to pick up.'

'Yeah,' said Lenny. 'Or who.'

It took eight hours to come through the mountains on the road to Oaxaca. It was a beautiful run of steep, cactus-sided precipices, roadside shrines, bleached-white crosses, under a clear blue sky. The big automobile meandered up and down the twisting mountain road of Mex 190, coming through and passing the occasional village where the villagers stopped, stared and crossed themselves as we drifted past trailing a long pall of dust in our wake. Oaxaca was the arts centre up in the mountains. Lenny wanted to have a look at some galleries and pick up some money from the American Express wire office, money he had saved while working back in New York. But the temperature inside the car was over 120 degrees, according to the little thermometer I'd bought back in a truck-stop in Alabama, and it was very uncomfortable.

'I swear to God I'm gonna die in this goddamn heat if we don't do something soon,' Lenny muttered.

'When the freeze is on the pumpkin,' said Tarris, 'it's no time for dicky dunkin'. But when it's hot 'n' sticky, it's time to dunk your dicky.'

'Very cute, Tarris,' said Lenny. 'But that doesn't really help right now, does it?'

'Next town we come to, bunje, stop at a cantina,' Tarris instructed. 'I'll fix us up.'

We motored a little while longer. Then we came to a little village. 'Here!' said Tarris, banging his fist on the dash. 'Pull over here, boy.'

I pulled over. We got out and stretched. Tarris walked

around to the rear, opened up the door and pulled out his canvas bag. Soon he found what he was looking for. Three pieces of colored cloth. He gave one to Lenny and one to myself.

'What's this?'

'This is a sarong. You wear it like a towel. Put it on. I'll go see if they'll sell me what we need.'

Tarris headed off to the *cantina* across the road.

He came back a few minutes later holding three small plastic bowls. Each bowl was filled with ice. He gave them to us.

'Old Sri Lankan remedy for the heat, boys. Fellas on the trains do it all the time over there, you know.'

'Do what?'

Tarris dunked his nuts.

It's not easy driving with your nuts in a bowl of ice. But when the air-conditioning isn't working, it is a great deal more comfortable.

16

Two days later we were back on the road, heading for the coast. 'Well,' Lenny asked me. 'Did you?'

'Did I what?' I asked.

'You know what I mean. Did you put the beasty to bed?'

Putting the beasty to bed was an expression for exorcizing the past. Not burning a candle for a loved one, but looking forward to meeting the next loved one. That sort of idea.

'With that nice lady?' I said. 'No, no, no. Just friends. What did you boys get up to?'

We were listening to 'Feliz Navidad', a salsa version of

'Merry Christmas' on a salsa erotica Christmas compilation tape. We bought it at a roadside *cantina*.

Tarris slapped his knee. 'It was hellish, wasn't it, Len?'

'Tarris,' said Lenny with a grin. 'I don't wanna hear you talk about it, alright?'

We were following in the wake of a Pemex petroleum tanker.

'But it's a beaut of a story, Len.'

'I don't fucking care.'

'You can tell me,' I said.

'I can,' said Lenny. 'But I ain't.'

'Why not?'

'Because it's kind of fucking embarrassing, if you want to know the truth. You want to tell the story, Tarris, go right ahead, but I ain't sayin' nothin'.'

'Good man,' said Tarris, rubbing his hands together. 'Picture this, bunje, ha ha. Me and Len, abandoned by our compadre, wandering about in a dark filthy part of town, two-thirty in the morning, when suddenly, shooting right across our bows, comes this fleet of – how would you care to describe 'em, Len?'

'I don't know, man. The light wasn't so good. But they looked kinda cute from where I was standing. Sexy.'

'Sexy? Ha ha! That is not how I'd care to describe 'em. Anyway, these young butterflies. What disgusting mouths! Fucky-sucky this, señor! Fucky-sucky that!'

'Yeah, it was great,' said Lenny.

'They were just interested in one thing and one thing only, Lenny.'

'Me.'

'No, not you. Your money, you bugger. That's all they wanted. Your pesos.'

'Tarris, you're a cynic. These little youngsters were just being pally. That's all. Nothin' more than that.'

'Pally?'

'Uh-huh.'

'So what happened?' I asked.

'He goes off and they get talking and it's not long before I hear him say, "Okay, ladies, how much?" "Twenty dollars," one girl says. To which Lenny – you got to love the boy's ambition – says, "What? For *all* of you? *All* night . . .?"'

'Hey,' said Lenny. 'Nothin' wrong with that, man. I was horny.'

'Doesn't finish there,' said Tarris with a nudge.

'I didn't think it would,' I said.

'The girls have a little pow-wow and they come up with what they think is the perfectly reasonable sum of one hundred dollars. "Tarris," Lenny says to me, "lend me the goddamn hundred dollars, will you?" And I say to him, "Are you sure about this, Len?" And he says, "Course I am, man. Just *look* at 'em!"'

'Well I did. But for the life of me I didn't get it. Four muscular young ladies. All in need of a good shave. But they did have the shoes with the bows on their toes.'

'So what happened?'

'I gave him the money and off they went, Lenny happier than a pig in fucking shit.'

'That's it?'

'No, the bugger's back, five minutes later, face white as a ghost, shouting, "Tarris, you motherfucking bastard – why didn't you tell me they were *men*!"'

'Jesus,' I said.

'I thought the language was a little ripe, too, bunje. And that was after I'd lent the bastard a hundred on good faith.'

'Hey,' said Lenny. 'How the hell was I supposed to know that these chicks had dicks?'

'They had mustaches, Len.'

'So what? I know a *lotta* nice girls with mustaches.'

17

Around seven-thirty we pulled into Salina Cruz, a big oil industry town on the coast. We found a bar near the main square and went inside. The air was still, sour and stale. The tables were metal, the bar wood, the floor a slab of red concrete. An old man shuffled in soon after, barefoot. He wore jeans and a shirt open to the waist. He had hammocks slung over his shoulder. The hammocks were tied carefully in a bundle.

'Hamacas?' he asked.

'No.'

'Muy barato!' the old man said. Very cheap. 'Mira!'

He got Lenny to get up out of his seat and hold one end as he untied the ball and stretched it out to its full length to show us.

'No, gracias,' said Lenny.

'Por qué?'

'Porque yo no quiero las hamacas,' said Lenny.

A purple mesh hammock was held up. 'Esta?'

Lenny shook his head.

The old man tossed the purple one on the floor, then picked up an orange and green one. 'Esta?'

'No.'

The old man tried Tarris.

'Cuanta costa?' Tarris asked.

'Veinte dollares, señor.'

'Veinte dollares!'

'Sí! Pero es muy barato, señor! Muy, muy barato!'

'If you'll take a few traveler's checks, I'll pay you the twenty.'

'Cheques de viaje? Sí! Claro, hombre. Passaporte?'

'Licencia Australian?'

'No!'

'Bugger!'

Back in the car, driving through town, it was dark.

'Was that you?' Tarris asked.

'Oh, man,' said Lenny. 'Open the windows. Smells like a sewage plant in here.'

But the smell was in the streets not the car. We lit lighters.

'Which way?' said Lenny.

'I'll get us out of here,' Tarris said.

'Why don't you drive and *I'll* get us out of here?' Lenny asked.

'I'm an expert at navigating,' said Tarris.

'Five-and-a-half hours to get out of Mexico City is not what I'd call ace navigating, pal. With all due respect.'

'That was different, Lenny.'

'How was it different?'

'We were pissed. Now pass us the map and slip on over,' said Tarris. 'What we need is the coast road.'

'There is *no* coast road on this map,' said Lenny.

'Believe me, they *always* have a coast road,' said Tarris. 'It's just not marked.'

We pulled away from the curb.

'The road we want,' said Tarris, pointing down a side street, 'is over there.'

'Down that little street?'

'Definitely.'

We bumped down the little street and some time later Lenny said, 'A brick wall. Nice navigating. Where next?'

'Left,' said Tarris, 'for the coast road.'

We went left but soon it, too, took a turn for the worst, becoming an uneven track.

'Just ahead before we pick up the main road,' said Tarris.

The sand track wound up and down for a while, then it thinned and finally stopped. So did we. The headlamps shone on a clump of brilliant green bushes.

'That,' said Tarris, 'was not meant to happen. Turn around. We'll ask in town.'

Back in town Tarris asked locals for the way, but the answer – it was the same the four times he asked – was a dismissive wave of the arm and the cry, 'Directo, hombre! Directo!' It didn't matter which way the car was pointed – north, south, east or west – the answer was always the same: 'Directo, hombre! Directo!'

Two hours later, we found the road out of town. A half-hour after that we came to a fork in the road with no sign-post.

'Left here,' said Tarris. 'Definitely left here, boys.'

We turned left. Three hours later Tarris said, 'Seem to be going back towards Oaxaca. Never mind. Turn round, I think.'

Lenny turned the car around on a precipitous dirt road, high up in the mountains.

'Nice navigating, Tarris,' said Lenny. 'That was about a what? A six-hour waste of time?'

Tarris chuckled. 'Not to worry, boys. Look at that fine view down the mountain! Ain't it a peach?'

An old truck roared past, lit up like a Christmas tree. It trailed a great plume of dust in its wake.

Tarris laughed. 'We'll have a little singsong. To lift the flagging spirits.'

'Cool, I'll start,' said Lenny.

'No you won't, I will,' I said.

But it was Tarris who started, and in a perfectly pitched lilting tenor he sang an old Cornish sea-song. It went like this:

> *Now a sailor and his true love were walking one day,*
> *Said the sailor to his true love, I'm bound far away,*
> *I'm bound for the Indies where the loud cannons roar,*
> *I must leave my Nancy, she's the girl I adore.*
>
> *Farewell, dearest Nancy, I can no longer stay*
> *For the top-sail is hoisted and the anchor is away*
> *And the good ship is waiting for the next rising tide*
> *And if ever I return, I will make you my bride.*

18

Seven o'clock the next morning I was sitting in the shade at a table in the small beach restaurant just along from where we had parked during the night, staring across the white sand at Lenny, over in the shallows, with his plaid pants rolled up above his hairy knees, in the middle of some strange morning ritual.

'What's he up to?' Tarris asked.

'I think maybe he's meditating.'

'That boy ain't religious. Mind you, he does drink enough.'

Shirt off, pasty chest and back bared to the sun, one-armed Ray-Bans perched on his ripening hooter, Lenny was standing in the water. His arms were raised, his fists closed except for the two index fingers which were both erect, describing two delicate circles. He stood immobile except for these two circling fingers, while the gentle surf lapped at his white legs and the hot morning sun beat down on the top of his curly brown head. We sat passing the bottle of Pepto back and forth, watching his actions as he kept his back to us, and his fingers twirling in the light breeze coming off the flat blue Pacific. Behind us two old queens sat in a huddle over the table, their arms around each other's shoulders. One was a bus conductor, the other worked for the city council.

Twirling and twitching as the flies tried to settle on his nose, Lenny continued this strange act in the hot, salty breeze. Then the activity suddenly ceased, the hands fell to his sides, the trunk swiveled, he fixed his one-armed sunglasses firmly on his face, exhaled heavily — as if he had completed a taxing circuit of the gym — and ran across the white sand towards us.

Lenny pulled out a chair and sat down.

'Is the sun getting to you, Len?' Tarris asked.

'What?'

'You feelin' alright there, boy?'

'Couldn't be better, man,' Lenny replied, shaking a cigarette loose from a packet on the table, sitting down, and then lighting it.

'Are you sure?'

'This place is really something, you know. Nice beach. Got the whole spot to ourselves. And to think I could be freezing my balls off back in Brooklyn. I gotta tell you, fellas, I'm almost happy my wife ran off with some goddamn herbal-tea-drinking, pick-up-driving asshole. It might have been the best thing to happen to me in a long time.'

'What were you doing just now?' I asked him. 'With your fingers?'

I showed him.

'That?' said Lenny.

'Yeah.'

'That was *exer*cises, man.'

'Exercises?'

'For the surfer bod. Chicks dig the surfer bod, you know what I mean? Now that we're here, time to get in shape.'

'Crap surf,' said Tarris, looking at the sea. 'After breakfast, I reckon we should go check the surf down at the point.'

Late that morning, we headed down the little dirt road to the point to see if there was any surf. We hadn't been going more than a few minutes when an old Toyota estate car came bouncing past, lifting great clouds of dirt, packed to the roof with family. It shot past us.

A mile later we passed parts of an exhaust. First a baffle. Then some brackets. Then some pipe. Then we came to the Toyota itself. The occupants, eight of them, were standing next to it.

We stopped to examine what was left of the exhaust. It was held together with welds and was split the length of it.

'Kaput,' I said to the woman.

'Sí,' the woman replied. 'Como mi esposo.'

Like her husband.

We asked if we could be of any assistance. The woman didn't think so. We set off. A little down the track we swept around a bend, the road fell away steeply and we smacked the underside of the car on a rock.

'Stop!' I said.

'Why?' asked Tarris.

'I didn't like the sound of that. I want to see if we broke anything.'

'Don't be bloody daft.'

'Stop the car. Let me take a look.'

Tarris braked. The dust rose, then settled.

'Turn the motor off,' I said.

'He's getting precious,' said Tarris. 'And I thought this was going to be the last reckless run before responsibilities and respectability ruined our little lives once and for all. Ah, well.'

Splaying on my belly in the hot dirt, I snaked under the hot metal at the front. There were no oil leaks. I worked my way out, stood up, dusted myself down and then got back in the car.

'Told you there was nothin' to worry about,' said Tarris. 'These Cadillacs are built like bloody tanks. Ain't that right, Len?'

'Yeah. And do me a favor, will ya?' said Lenny. 'Lighten the fuck up. This is meant to be fun.'

'You're right,' I said.

'That's better!' said Tarris. 'Now slide over there, bunje, and let me treat you both to a dazzling display of wheelmanship.'

I moved over. Tarris slid into the driver's seat. Then he turned the motor over.

But it didn't start.

Crawling under the front end of the car, Tarris shouted, 'I see what the problem is. Nothin' to worry about. Come here. Let me teach you a little trick I learned when I was thirteen. And bring a screwdriver, will you? The one with the flat head.'

I picked up the screwdriver from the back and worked my way under the front of the car. I passed the screwdriver to Tarris.

'Lovely job,' said Tarris. 'But wipe that smirk off your lips, it doesn't suit you.'

Tarris put the screwdriver up to the round lump of the

starter motor, placing the flat metal bar across the breadth of it.

'Now tell that git to turn it over.'

Lenny turned the motor over. The electric switching gear clicked once, twice, then a bright shower of white and yellow sparks rained down on us.

'Oh Jesus!' said Tarris.

Gears whirred, then the motor fired and roared. We crawled out and stood up and dusted the sand off us.

'Nice job,' I said.

'You can thank the owners of The Poldark Inn for that. If I wanted to go disco on a Friday night, I had to steal the parents' car. Buggers wouldn't gimme the keys.'

'Why not?'

'I was only twelve at the time.'

We got back in the car and set off. There was no surf at the point. In fact, there was no point. We found a lagoon where some fishing smacks were moored.

'Stay one day here, boys,' Tarris announced. 'Then I reckon we should tip for Salvador.'

'*Salvador?*' Lenny asked.

'Yas.'

'Isn't there like, you know, *death* squads and shit down in Salvador?'

'*Was,*' said Tarris. 'Not any more, Len. Death squads are finished with.'

'Oh, good.'

'Now there just be the civil war, of course. From what I understand that's only in the *northern* part of the country. But it says here in the book that if you go to the tourist agency in the capital, San Salvador, they'll tell you where the war zones are.'

'I'm not goin' through a war zone,' said Lenny. 'You idiots want to go, you can go on your own, but you can count me out.'

Tarris wasn't listening.

'Salvador – that's the place for us. Pumping surf in Salvador. Not like this fucking shite.'

'Look,' said Lenny. 'Why don't we skip Salvador, cruise through Honduras, then slip into Nicaragua without any of the hassle?'

'Can't do that,' said Tarris, shaking his head vehemently.

'Why *not*?'

'Crap surf in Honduras. Beach break. Not worth the trip. Besides, San Salvador, I hear, is rocking.'

'It is?' I asked.

'The dog's bollocks, bunje. Clubs, bars, girlies, dancing –'

'Well, that's that, then,' I said.

'What's *what*?' said Lenny.

'We're going to Salvador.'

'Why?' Lenny asked. 'To go fucking surfing?'

'As noble a cause as any,' said Tarris.

On the way back to town we met an old, dusty gray Ford Econoline van. It had three occupants, two women and a man. We flagged them down. They didn't know anything about surfing conditions here, or any other place up or down the coast. But they had seen us pull in next to them on the beach at three in the morning and we'd given them a fright. They invited us to follow them down the road to have a beer or two at one of the *cooperativas* in the next village.

That evening we dined with them.

Jerry was a waiter from San Francisco and being in the food business was a food expert. He ordered for the table.

Harriet and Susan were from Canada. They were lovers. We ate at an empty restaurant just down from where we were all parked. We ate a platter of shrimp and garlic. At dinner Susan, the younger and prettier of the two ladies, treated us all to a lecture on hygiene habits to be observed by travelers in the Third World. Only eat fruits you can peel or vegetables that are fried. Make sure all meat is cooked thoroughly. Be careful to wash hands before and after every meal. Only drink water from a bottle. Take fifteen types of malaria pill. Coat the body in sun block, bug block. And so on. Susan was an expert on health and Lenny found her elfish looks extremely attractive after five beers. Whispered in my ear, just as Jerry was telling us all about a mystical out-of-body experience he'd had in a cave near Merida, 'Going to try and be the third wheel in that Econoline tonight.'

'You haven't got a hope in hell,' I told him. 'They're lesbians.'

'So what, man? I *love* lesbians.'

When the beer was finished and Susan had run out of things to lecture us all about, and Jerry had eaten all the shrimp heads on the platter and told us about his upcoming trip into Guatemala to see the ruins, the city of Antigua and Lake Chichicastenango, and Tarris and Harriet had traded insults, we walked down the beach, barefoot, to watch Lenny dance. He performed on the hood of the hearse.

Lenny squatted and slid forward. He swiveled his hips and shuffled backwards. He performed a number of daring 360 degree toe-spin pirouettes. And it was all going near perfect as far as I could judge – pirouettes, surfer-shuffle, all of it – until he made a small error of judgement. He moved the act to the roof.

'Be careful!' Susan shouted.

'Break a leg!' Harriet barked huskily.

But Lenny didn't hear. Snapping his fingers, shaking his hips, he was lost in music. From one side of the roof to the other he pranced, while we stood on the sand, some six feet below, and watched.

Then he fell off the roof. This was not part of the act. When we strolled round the side to find him, he was curled up in the sand, clutching his ribs, moaning.

'Are you alright, Lenny?' Tarris giggled. 'Talk to us, boy!'

But all Lenny could get out was this soft whistling and bubbling sound.

'My ribs,' Lenny groaned, 'I think I bust . . .'

'Don't be daft,' said Tarris. 'Not with as much drink as you've had. You're just winded. That's all.'

'You don't understand . . . I've really . . . Oh, *man*, this hurts.'

'Well, that was a *very* silly thing to do, *wasn't* it?' Susan said.

'Yeah,' said Harriet. 'Fucking typical.'

Tarris bent over.

'Let me get a look. There you go. C'mon, now, boy. Roll over.'

'Does he know what he's doing?' Susan asked me.

'Probably not.'

Tarris chortled merrily to himself as he examined the patient.

'Where did he learn first aid?' Susan asked me.

'On the farm,' I replied.

Lenny groaned. Susan squatted next to Tarris.

'What d'you know about first aid?'

I could see his patience was being taxed. But he answered civilly.

'I spent ten years in mining camps in the jungle and deserts of this world. I've seen limbs caught in chains and mangled in winch gear. I've put splints on legs where the bones have come through the skin. I've helped dress men with burns all over their body. This man is drunk, Susan. That's all.'

Susan huffed.

Tarris poked Lenny.

'That hurt, bastard?'

'What do you think?' I asked.

'Just bruising.'

'How do you *know* it's just bruising? I say we take Lenny to a hospital!'

'Good idea,' said Tarris. 'And what hospital might that be?'

'There must be a hospital around here *some*where.'

'This is Mexico, my darlin'. Not Canada.'

'I'm not your darling,' said Susan.

'Yeah, and you start that shit,' said Harriet, pointing her skull ring at Tarris, 'and I'll slap ya.'

We fed Lenny Tylenol, loaded him carefully into the back of the hearse and left him curled up on the futon, cradling his shoulder and ribs. We would not be able to move Lenny for another two days. Another valuable lesson learned for the road: dancing drunk on the car is as dangerous as driving drunk. This was also banned forthwith.

19

Mex 200 is the main road on the Pacific coast to Guatemala. To give our invalid some room to be comfortable, Tarris lay across the partition behind the bench seat like a big cat, his hands interlinked on his chest, his wraparound reflector glasses perched on his broken nose while I drove. Lenny was silent, staring out of the open window from behind his broken sunglasses, a bottle of half-finished tequila in his lap.

'This is bullshit. Maybe I should fucking leave you guys and fly home.'

'Stop your whingeing,' said Tarris.

'Whingeing? Now what is whingeing?'

'Whingeing is whining,' I translated.

'I'm not whining. I'm just telling you guys, maybe it'd be a lot better if I . . .'

'You should count yourself lucky it's only your ribs.'

'Hey,' said Lenny. 'It doesn't *get* more painful than this, pal. This is fuckin' *killin'* me.'

'Ribs aren't that bad,' said Tarris. 'Not as bad as some places.'

'How do you know? Have you ever broken a rib, Tarris?'

'I have.'

'Yeah? How many?'

'Ten. No, I lie. Eleven. In a mining accident.'

'Eleven? Jeez. What happened? A pipe fall on you?'

'No, a jeep, actually.'

'A jeep?'

'Yeah. Rolled the bastard on the way back to camp after a night in town. But even that, Lenny, even that was nothin' compared to this thing I got back in, let me think now, must be, ehm, 'seventy-four. Yeah. That was it. Nineteen seventy-four. The most savage pain I have ever experienced in my life, Len. And I've had a few. Oh yes, indeed.'

'I got a feeling you're going to tell us about it.'

'Only if you want to hear it, boys. Only if you want to hear —'

'No, go on. You got this far,' said Lenny. 'Let's hear the rest of it.'

Tarris lit his cigarette.

'Ehm, well let me see now. I was on a job up in the jungles of Borneo, for a petroleum company, I reckon. And I musta bin headin' back up river with my guide after two weeks R&R in the Philippines when I, ehm, came down with it.'

'A stomach thing?' asked Lenny.

'Much worse.'

'A fever?'

'Oh, I had a fever alright, but that wasn't the pain.'

'So what was it?'

'My penis. The thing was on *fire*, Lenny. I musta caught, ehm, something from the . . . Anyway, there I was, up a river, in the middle of a stinking jungle, five days from camp, no medical supplies, and each time I got to go for a piss, I'm pissing napalm.'

'Jesus! So what the hell did you do?' Lenny asked.

'I got on the radio and called base. That's what I did. I told 'em to get a chopper in the air and fly me up some drugs. But here's where my problems start. The radio op is not my regular man. He's a little villager, nice chap, but he hardly speaks a word of the Queen's English. Still, I try and explain things as best I can and hope the man has understood me. So, one day passes – no chopper. Another day passes. Still no chopper. A *third* day passes and by this time I'm almost delirious, Len. I'm in a pain that you could not possibly im*agine* . . .'

'No,' said Lenny. 'No, I think I can.'

'Luckily, on the morning of the fourth day I hear the whup-whup of the company chopper . . .'

'So they got to you before the old pecker fell off, huh?'

'Well, not quite – but I'll get to that. When the pilot lands I discover he hasn't brought me my penicillin like I asked. He's come with two *Playboys*, a copy of the Bible, and a small jar of Vick's Vapor Rub for a bad chest cold . . .'

Lenny slumped into a heavy silence.

'How long was it before you developed this pain?'

'Four days. That's why I always travel with a well-stocked bag of pharmaceuticals. Just in case, you see.'

'Tarris, you mind if I ask you a personal question?' Lenny asked.

'Not at all, Len.'

'Are you circumcised?'

'Had to be after that. Horrible, it was. Lying there on the doc's operating table, in the middle of the jungle, looking up at this brown face reminding him for the hundredth time, "Remember, Doc, it's circumcision, *not* bloody castration . . ."'

We didn't hear another word of complaint from Lenny from that moment on.

20

Pushing further south, the Mexican countryside changed. It got greener. We passed a few old pick-up trucks, their beds loaded high with green bananas ripening in the hot sun. We passed old men on donkeys, wearing white smocks, with brown sun-crinkled faces, large straw hats and holding sticks. We passed young barefoot kids standing by the roadside holding the tails of large iguanas for sale. We smelled the fresh smell of just-fallen rain on hot earth. And we sat and we sweated because nobody could sell us any ice to put in our bowls.

Around two in the afternoon we came to a bridge where men were working. A man waved a red cloth to stop us. He pointed to the side of the road. Then he fired something off in rapid Spanish which I could not understand.

'Lentamente, por favor,' I said.

No puedes something else, he said, wiping the beads of sweat off his forehead with a tattered red rag. 'Por dos horas!'

'They're having to do some structural repairs on the bridge,' Lenny said, adjusting his sling. 'Guy says it's going to take a coupla hours until they get things straightened out here.'

'Bugger me,' said Tarris. 'How'd you know that?'

'When you're lying on your back all day, you got to do *something*, Tarris.'

'A talent for languages,' said Tarris. 'Not so bloody useless after all.'

'Let's pay the man,' I said.

'Won't work,' said Lenny. 'They already got a 'dozer on the bridge.'

Tarris slid out from his perch on the partition and yawned. 'Two hours? Could be two days by the time these buggers are done. Let's walk the ford and see what the conditions offer.'

Lenny started laughing. 'You wanna ford the river in *this*?'

'Why not?'

Tarris opened the side door and was off, ambling towards the steep dirt track at the river's edge, humming a tune as the pick-ups slipped past him, going in and muddying the clear-watered, fast-moving river.

I walked over to the bridge. Down at the river Tarris stood for a minute, rubbing his square, stubbly chin. He took his flops off, held them in his hand, then waded barefoot into the river. He walked slowly over, then slowly back, stopping here and there to prod at something underfoot. The inspection took ten minutes. When done, he stood for a minute and studied the vehicles: where they went in, where they went over, and how they came out.

'Reckon you shouldn't get stuck.'

'What does that mean?'

'It means we should get a move on and stop wasting so much bloody time, bunje.'

I looked down at the river. It looked a little deep and a little fast. I looked at my hearse. Even with the limousine air-shocks and the coil-spacer kit for the front end it was still only a hearse, a city and highway dweller; it was not one of those all-terrain vehicles that were dropping in and ploughing across river with a fair amount of ease.

'Maybe we should wait,' I said.

One of the men had lowered a fishing-line and hook into the water. Others sat in the shade having lunch.

'Could be hours,' said Tarris. I walked up to the old man sitting on the curbside, fanning himself with his red flag. I asked him how long he might be.

He shrugged.

I asked him if the work would be completed today.

He shrugged and spat.

'Well?' Tarris asked, coming over.

'He doesn't know when they're going to be finished.'

'I say we try it.'

'What if we get stuck?'

'Stuck? That's not a problem, bunje. Problem is getting swept *away*. Then, well – we're buggered. But in my opinion it's not fast or high enough to get swept away. Anyway, if we get stuck I'll just get one of the lads to give us a tow.'

He pointed at an old man with three donkeys.

I reversed past the long line of cars that had decided not to attempt to cross and joined the line of four-wheels that were dipping over the hill, to bump down the steep dirt track and roll into the fast-moving water.

Tarris scurried down the bank, laughing to himself. A crowd from the taco, soda and tortilla kiosk filed out on to the bridge to lean over the parapet and watch. At the bottom I stopped. The river looked faster than it had from above. And deeper. When the truck in front of me, a big Chevrolet Silverado, got stuck halfway across, I had second thoughts, but by this time there was a long line of trucks behind. The Silverado started again and cleared the river.

'C'mon, you bugger!' Tarris shouted. 'Let's be having you! And remember – keep the speed up and keep them wheels turning, but *not* spinning!'

I let off the foot brake and squeezed the gas. The front wheels edged into the river. Then the back. We moved slowly out into the stream. The water was as high as the door jambs. But the car didn't stop and didn't drift. It continued to push across. Soon we were halfway.

'Get on, bee!' Tarris shouted.

Bumping up the other side, the river gushing out of the wheel wells as the hearse clawed up the steep yellow sand track, I had to smile.

I parked on the roadside at the top and got out.

Lenny came over and patted the hood. 'Looks like we don't need that four-wheel after all,' he drawled, with a big grin. 'I'll be damned.'

21

We stopped in the small border town of Hidalgo at dusk. It was Saturday night. The main square formed the business and cultural hub of the place. There were flower stores and ice-cream parlors, shoe and clothing stores with an old bandstand in the middle. The town was pretty. In the branches of pecan trees were fairy lights. We found a little restaurant called China-Mex just off the square. The owner came to the table. We ordered chow-mein.

The lady couldn't do it. She fanned herself and said something rapidly which Lenny then translated – forbidden to cook Chinese when the husband was not there. Her husband was Chinese. He wouldn't allow it because she wasn't very good at it. Today the man was over in Guatemala buying auto supplies, so all she could offer was a *quesadilla* – a cheese tortilla; *pollo* – chicken; or a bifsteak.

We ordered chicken and beer. Tarris, who had been silent for some time, suddenly shot to his feet and went off. Fifteen minutes later he returned excited and agitated.

'I've seen something,' he announced. 'Something . . . Eee!'

'What's up with him?' Lenny asked.

A young woman had caught Tarris's eye. And because of her we didn't get into the hearse and slip out of town on our way to the border, a few kilometers away, after dinner. He wouldn't allow it. He was feeling romantic. He wished to express his feelings to the young lady. We obliged him.

'What do you want to tell her?' I asked.

He thought about it. Then his eyes lit up. 'Translate this, bunje: To the maid with the skin as soft as a she-mouse's belly –'

'She-mouse's *what*?' said Lenny, spitting into his beer.

'Belly,' said Tarris.

'You wanna tell this chick she's got the hide of a rodent?'

'I wanna tell her her skin is as soft as a she-mouse's belly. That's what I want to tell her.'

'I don't know, man. It may be different where you come

from. But you tell some chick in Brooklyn she's got the skin of a rodent, she's gonna smack you. It's a fact.'

'El vientre de una ratona!' I said, looking up from my pocket dictionary.

'El vientre de una ratona?' Tarris murmured with a smile. 'Beautiful. *Beau*tiful. Now the rest, please, if you wouldn't mind.'

'What rest?'

'The compliments of Mr Tarris Hill.'

'He's serious about this?' said Lenny.

'I think so.'

'Well?'

'Los complimentos de Señor Tarris Hill.'

'Write it out for me, bunje. All of it.'

I wrote it out on the back of a paper napkin. Tarris held it carefully in his hand. He tried different readings. When satisfied, he tilted his California Angels baseball cap to one side, brushed the dirt from his Mambo T-shirt and said, 'Vamanos, amigos.'

Dusk was descending quickly on the town's square. Young men on bicycles rode past. We walked through the square and took a seat on a park bench. Tarris strolled over to the door of the little corner store on his own. He had some flowers in one hand and the napkin in the other. We watched him enter. Then we watched him read it to her.

It worked. The young lady put her head in her hands, blushed and laughed. Tarris handed her the flowers, bowed deeply, then kissed her hand and retreated. Not bad for an old fart.

On the way out of town Lenny said, 'So where did a rough little country boy like you learn to be the Don Juan? I'll tell you, man, that girl lapped it up.'

'I like romance,' said Tarris.

And as we drove along the dark road to the border at Talisman, under a bright firmament of shining, shooting stars, Tarris told us a little love story. About himself as it turned out.

'A courtship like this happens just once in a lifetime, boys,' he said. 'If you're lucky.'

'Let's hear it.'

'It musta bin ten years ago now when I first heard about her, this lovely maid who had just moved to the north coast. My friend Arkwright told me about her. He said she was the most beautiful woman he'd seen in Cornwall for a long, long time. Well, pickings had been slim that winter so I thought I'd better have a look. Next day I made an appointment at the salon where she was cutting hair and the minute I walked into the salon, I heard the most wonderful laugh. Peals of it. Sweet, sweet laughter filling the salon. And of course it was her. She was *just* like Arkwright had said –'

'Beautiful?'

'Took my breath away.'

'What'd she look like?'

'About five-eight. Freckles. Auburn hair cut in a fringe. Bright and lively little eyes, a beautiful, happy face – she had a rare and glorious beauty. I was taken with her the first minute I saw her. Anyway, as I sat in the barber's chair and admired her in the mirror, I discovered many things. She was newly divorced. She had children. A nice old house in town. She liked her job. She liked to play tennis and golf and have dinner with her girlfriends and, best of all –'

'She didn't have a boyfriend?'

'She didn't have a boyfriend.'

'Go on.'

'Well, anyway, when she was finished doing my hair, I asked her if she would like to come out with me for an evening.'

'So you got a date,' said Lenny. 'What did you do on this date?'

'Well, if there's one fact I've learned after forty-two years on this planet, it's this: women, they love a nice romantic surprise.'

'You little rascal,' I said.

'I fixed a date with her. I told her if she wouldn't mind I should like to surprise her. She said that would be very nice. So, a couple of days later, I send a taxi to pick her up from her work in town. I give the driver instructions to bring her out to the country but not say a word about her final destination as I want it to be a surprise. He picks her up. She gets in the taxi. They set off into the countryside and as luck would have it, it was one of those Cornish summer's eves that are magic. The lanes were filled with wild flowers, the sheep and the cows were grazing peacefully in the valley, the old sea was quiet and peaceful, and the light was crisp and clean. Half-hour later, the taxi arrives at the gate of a field I own. Tethered to this gate I have my horse Cracker-Jack. The taxi-driver tells her to get up on Crackers because Crackers knows where he's going. This, of course, is new to her, but she opens the gate, untethers the horse, climbs up on his back and the two of them head up the valley. Sunset on horseback, heading up a lovely valley to meet a strange man. Better than a pasty and a pint. By the time my old horse appears at the top field, she's flushed and quite touched by it all, I can tell. I'm waiting for her, dressed in my DJ and wellington boots. I have a candle-lit table set under the shade of a big oak and in the brook nearby I have a bottle of Chilean Champagne from Ivor . . .'

'That's *beautiful*. And this is true?'

'On my life. I had Arkwright come and play his mandolin as the moon rose slow over my farm while we ate.'

'Tell me something, Tarris?' Lenny asked.

'What?'

'Did you get in her pants that night?'

'That,' said Tarris, 'would be telling now, wouldn't it?'

'So where's she now?'

'She's in Cornwall.'

'Why aren't you back there with her?'

'I gave the woman seven years to marry me and for seven years I was true to her. Seven years were up a week before this bugger called.'

22

'AMIGO! ... AMIGO! ... DINERO! ... AMIGO!' they started hollering as soon as we rolled to a halt in a cloud of dust at the end of a long line of cars waiting for the border to open around seven the next morning.

'Ah,' said Tarris with a grin. 'Opportunity knocks. Excuse me.'

A mob of sweating men with briefcases, money-belts, pocket calculators, crucifixes and other bits of gold surrounded Tarris.

'Quieres cambiar los cheques de via-hairos?' he asked.

They all did.

'You,' Tarris said pointing at a man with a big gap in his front teeth. 'Quieres cambiar cheques?'

'Sí, hombre!'

Tarris pulled out a wad of checks and the man turned his calculator on.

'Por dollares, cuanto quetzales?' Tarris asked.

The little calculator was fingered. The screen was lifted and waved. Tarris studied it. 'That's ten percent less than I'd get at the bank, you little monkey!' he said.

The man shrugged.

'What about you?'

Another screen was lifted and displayed.

'That is what I call thievery. I reckon you boys can do a lot better than that. '

'No!' said one.

'No!' they all echoed indignantly.

'Fair dinkum. Who wants eight hundred dollars?'

All of them wanted it.

'Excell-entay. Licencia Australian?'

'No!'

'Ah well,' said Tarris, 'maybe next time.'

One hour later the border opened and the place was hot, dusty and noisy with pedestrian traffic. Women walked barefoot carrying goods in colorful woven bags on their heads. There was a line a quarter-mile long of cars towing new cars to take home to sell, cars towing wrecks to sell, and cars just heading south with Mexican, Nicaraguan or Guatemalan plates. We walked down the road to the bridge. In fifteen minutes – it was always easier to get out of one place than get in – the car and immigration documents had the right exit stamps and we were free to drive across the bridge to the Guatemalan checkpoint.

Men were waiting for us with spray nozzles and plastic tanks.

'Fumigación, señor!' a man said, leaning through the

window and having a little scout to see what might be of value.

'Him,' said Tarris, pointing at Lenny.

'I love you, too,' said Lenny.

The man spied the cigarettes. 'Marl-boro para mí, sí?' he asked.

Lenny gave him a Marlboro.

'Un otro para mi amigo?'

'No, beat it.'

'Okay.'

We got out. He sprayed the car. Another pack of entrepreneurs found us.

'Lovely job,' said Tarris, rubbing his hands together. 'Aquí, gentlemen.'

No luck there either.

Lenny had been talking with a tall, skinny man with a mustache. He came over. 'This guy,' Lenny said, 'says you won't be able to get the car through unless he helps you. He says it's a very busy day today. However, if you go with him, he knows how to get the job done fast.'

'Sí, sí,' said the man. 'Rápido, hombre. No problema para el gringo! No problema!'

'How much?' I asked.

'Poquito,' he said, grinning, showing me a small gap between thumb and forefinger.

The line was not moving. The man in the kiosk was talking to his friend. I gave the mustache man my documents.

'Marlboro?' he asked.

I gave him a cigarette.

'Fuego?'

I gave him a light.

'Venga, hombre!'

My guide didn't pay notice to the line waiting at the window. He elbowed his way in ahead of an old man in a straw hat and said something to the officer. The officer ignored him. The old man shoved my guide to one side. My guide shoved the old man out of the way. I asked for my papers back.

He waggled his finger in my face. 'No!'

'Por qué?'

'Porque es mejor si yo lo hago por el señor. Mucho, mucho mejor! Y más rápido también.'

He turned his head and presented the papers. This time the passports were studied. My man smiled as if to say, 'You see? You see what I can do for you?'

But the officer shook his head and told him we couldn't pass into Guatemala unless we had the right stamp in our passports from the Guatemalan consul back in Tapachula. Anybody wanting to enter Guatemala had to have a stamp from the consul. This is not what it said in the guide-book. I showed him what it said in the guide-book. He didn't give two shakes what it said in the guide-book. If we wanted to drive through Guatemala, we needed a stamp from the consul and that was the end of it.

'You like a Marlboro?' I said.

He did. But it didn't make any difference. No stamp, no visiting Guatemala. My guide now asked me for his cut.

'Por qué?'

He grinned.

'What's the crack?' said Tarris, walking over.

I explained.

'Nine o'clock on a Sunday morning – what consulate's going to be open nine o'clock on a Sunday bloody morning?'

23

A tousled chubby head with mustache and a puzzled look poked out of a second-story window of a little house with gate and rose garden up in the small town of Tapachula, back up from the border station, in Mexico.

We'd caught a cab from the bridge with two Salvadorians, Luis and Freddy, auto mechanics living in Texas but born in El Salvador. They were heading home in two combis with their families to visit relatives, sell the cars, and make money. They explained to the face in the window that we were all in transit to El Salvador, but had been instructed to come up here to get a stamp to pass through Guatemala.

'Ah!' The man smiled. 'Momentito, por favor!'

A couple of minutes later a heavy little man in tight spandex bicycle shorts, velveteen slippers and a white cotton singlet and robe appeared. This was the honorable consul for Guatemala. We followed him down the garden path and through the front door of the consulate where it was cool. He took our passports, went to a big dark wood desk in the middle of the large room and asked us to sit on the chairs against one wall.

Forty-five minutes later we were back on the bridge. Lenny had met a man called Francisco. Francisco was a Salvadorian national who had fled his homeland in the early 1980s because of the death squads and gone north to the United States. He had been deported twice. Only two days ago he'd been caught making his way through Mexico and deported to Guatemala. Now he was waiting for the lunch hour when the border guards took a siesta. Then he could wade across the river and sneak back into Mexico. Once across, he hoped to hop freights north to Juma, California, then more freights up and across to Denver where he had a wife and children. Francisco didn't have one cent to his name. He had what he wore. He was going to beg for food on his journey. But he was incredibly cheerful for a man so destitute. His final destination was Canada. A Salvadorian lawyer in Quebec had set up a job placement scheme for Salvadorians. The government would give them a small amount of money and get them started with a new life. Francisco wanted to have his own garage. He had been beaten up and robbed in Mexico when they caught him in a train yard. But he spoke English, loved Marlboros, and was kind to us. He told me it would cost only six quetzals for fumigation, then sixteen quetzals for a *transmigrante* pass, and finally another forty quetzals for the little green decal that goes in the windshield of every vehicle in transit through Guatemala.

In one hour our papers were processed, and we left Francisco with some money and cigarettes and followed Freddy and Luis in their combis. At the top of the pass we came to a checkpoint. Two sullen adolescents in army greens gestured for us to park. We pulled over. Luis and Freddy were summoned inside the hut to show their papers. When they were finished, I went in. Luis said, 'Maybe I should come with you. He not a good guy.'

I showed the soldier my papers. He asked me for a donation.

'For what?'

He smiled.

'Give him a quetzal. Make him happy.'

One quetzal was about twenty-five cents. I gave him a quetzal. It didn't make him at all happy. In fact, it pissed him off. He slung it back at me and shouted something at the soldiers standing nearby.

'Mierda,' said Luis.

The soldiers searched the combis. When the contents had been emptied on the roadside, the young soldiers went back and slumped against a tree. The chief instructed Luis and Freddy to pack the vans quick before he gave them a fine for littering. They didn't search the hearse. He wanted to make a point. Don't help gringos.

'Welcome to Latin America,' said Tarris. 'But you know what, boys? Let this be a lesson. Next time we have to give money, we mustn't insult them with a tiny sum. We must be generous. Give the fat bastards a dollar. You might find the experience rewarding. I always have.'

24

We followed Freddy and Luis on fast, freshly paved black-tops. We stopped for lunch at a roadside *cantina* and ate chicken. By nine that night the tarmacadam stopped abruptly and we flew on to a dust road. Stones ricocheted off the hearse's underbelly as the headlamps picked a path through the dust kicked up in the wake of the combis of Luis and Freddy.

A mad old woman wearing a sheet over her head stood in the middle of the road. She had her arms outstretched and was not moving. She was miles from anywhere and I almost hit her.

Minutes later we were there, border number three, Valle Nuevo. We swept down a long hill toward the faint colored lights and a small town in the distance. But we had learned a useful lesson at Talisman. Money-changers – border dogs was Lenny's description of them – were to be discouraged.

Always wanting money. Never taking no for an answer. So this time, when we rolled down the hill to the customs shed at the bottom and the pack came running down the hill after us, yelling for our custom, we were ready for them.

We got out.

'Hola,' I said.

A pack of eight overweight men waving calculators came to a grinding halt.

'Ai! Ai! Ai!' one said.

'Son funerarios!' said another.

We were in full dress: top hats, long coats, white gloves. Dashing.

'Ehm,' said Tarris with a big smile. 'Quieres cambiar the old dinero? . . . Cheques viajeros?'

Nothing.

'Well, well, well. Flummoxed. The lot of them. What a bunch of big bubbas.'

The group inched closer, staring at us, then at the dusty hearse parked behind.

'Es una carroza!'

'Es una puta madre de carroza!'

Just then a small pair of brown hands appeared on the legs of one of the men standing at the front of the group. They tugged and the legs moved to one side. A little man appeared. Short black hair, no shoes, a tattered T-shirt, big brown eyes and dark brown skin.

'Es tu carro, señor?' he asked.

'Sí,' I replied.

'Donde vas?'

'Salvador.'

He nodded sagely. 'Si tu vas a Salvador, señor, creo que tu debes comprar un poco de dinero, sí?'

So we changed money with the little man. His name was Hector and he was about nine years old.

25

Across the large dust lot from the customs and immigration huts was a *cantina* with shutters that slapped in the wind. A storm was blowing in.

'What'd I tell you, boys, eh?' said Tarris. 'What'd I tell you? There must be the mother of depressions out there. That's what we're getting licked with down here. You know what that means, don't you?'

'Yeah, we gotta buy an umbrella,' said Lenny.

'Lots of lovely swell. Be slicing down the waves tomorrow.'

Tarris was very excited. In the guide-book it said there was excellent surf.

'What d'you want to eat?' I asked.

'I'll do a quick recce and have a chat with the guard. See if we're going to need to get a stamp from the consul to get in. By the way, have either of you boys made a will? No. Oh. Well, it's something to think about. Get me some sea-chicken. Or the bifsteak and chips.'

Tarris wandered off towards the border. We walked across the lot to the *cantina*. Tumbleweed bounced over the dirt. Dust devils spun and darted and then collapsed in the dark. An old Freightliner cab-over with one working headlamp, pulling a flat-bed trailer loaded high with coconuts, pulled into the lot and parked next to a big Suburban towing a trailer with six eighteen-foot fishing boats bound for the Lago in Nicaragua. The air-brakes let out a tired whoosh and the driver jumped down and scratched himself.

Freddy, Luis and their families laid their food out on the concrete inspection benches to eat. We ate with our banker, Hector, and his friends Nissin and Jorge.

The *cantina* was small. A hurricane lamp swung in the wind from a hook above the bar. The young Guatemalan woman entertained some of her admirers – thin, goofy-looking men who scowled at us and slapped Hector around the head a couple of times. We ordered bifsteak, *patatas fritas* and sodas. Halfway through dinner, Tarris walked back in, grinning.

'Good news, boys,' he said. 'No need for papers from the consul. I spoke to the guard over in Salvador. Don't need a stamp.'

'Sure,' said Lenny. 'That's because the government is trying to *encourage* tourism, Tarris. Salvador, you see, is gonna be the next Florida. They got condos, time-shares, golf –'

Tarris grinned. 'You're going to like this one, Len.'

'I doubt it.'

'They got a sign on the bridge: Bienvenidos a El Salvador!'

'So?'

'It's peppered with bullet holes.'

Late that night I woke up. It was hot on the front seat of the hearse. Lenny had the bed in the back. I had the windows closed because of bugs. We were going to take it in turns on the front seat, I'd have a few hours, then Tarris. I sat up. Tarris and Luis's son were sitting on the inspection bench looking up at the stars. Tarris was smoking and pointing out the different stars and constellations to the young boy. I listened for a bit and smiled. The boy had a fierce curiosity. They covered a vast territory of science, ending up on relativity, quasars and black holes.

I went back to sleep. That night was the first night I stopped thinking of home. Home was now where the hearse was.

26

Entering El Salvador is easy. The men seemed pleased to see us. The only stipulation for entry was that we took the *Comandante*'s good friend, a policeman, with us to San Salvador, the capital, a four-hour drive away. Lenny was not fond of this idea.

'Bad karma,' he said.

'Vamos a la playa a La Libertad,' I explained to the *Comandante*. 'No vamos a San Salvador.'

The *Comandante* had an answer to that one.

Lenny said, 'He says we're going to San Salvador. Or we ain't going nowhere.'

We put the *Comandante*'s friend in the back and made a little seat for him on the futon which was rolled up. Then we set off. The low had gone through and the weather had cleaned itself up. It was hot and blue and clear.

There was no road for the first forty-five kilometers inland from the frontier. It was a sand and dirt track. Sometimes with holes so deep you could bury an axle. This often caused radical maneuvers using the breadth of the track to skirt round the many holes, which created confusion when oncoming traffic had the same idea. But it was interesting driving. Nobody paid any attention to the normal rules of engagement. You overtook on the inside, the outside, you passed oncoming cars and overloaded buses and produce-trucks to the left, right – it didn't matter as long as you missed them and the big craters in the road – if you could see the road. Half the time you couldn't because of the thick curtain of dust which hung in the air, lifted by anything that drove or walked over this two-car-wide track bordered by dense, tropical undergrowth.

After an hour of bouncing around, passing through little villages, the road came to a T-junction and a beautiful strip of clear black macadam. On the opposite side of the road was a Texaco station. We pulled into the station, filled up, hosed the car down and bought sodas. Oil traces fanned around the whitewall tire, front-left side. I wiped it down and did not think any more of it. An hour later, after we waved goodbye to Freddy and Luis and their families, a bullock walked out in front of the car. I hit the brakes, the brakes went soft and the steering-wheel vibrated furiously.

'What was that?'

'That'll be your wheel-bearings,' said Tarris, lying on his back, in his usual spot, on the partition. 'Or a steering bushing.'

'Is it hard to fix?'

'Not if you got the parts.'

27

Standing at the counter of the bank the next morning, watching his money being counted, Lenny leaned over and said to me, 'You see that?'

'See what?'

'She's not married.'

'So?'

'She's a little cutie, huh?'

A bundle of money was pushed forward over the counter with a passport and a white form to be signed.

'Very pretty.'

'Señorita?' said Lenny.

'Qué?'

'Quieres, ah, comer con mi esta noche?'

'What's the boy up to?' Tarris asked.

'Trying to get a date,' I said.

'Ha ha ha,' Tarris laughed. 'Ha ha ha! Just look at the state of him!'

Lenny was in his beach outfit: cut-off trousers falling apart at the seam. Dusty workboots coming apart at the sole. Guyana is Moving! T-shirt with about a million creases.

The teller looked up.

Lenny smiled and leaned further over the counter. 'Pienso que tu es muy guapa, muy bellissima y yo quiero comer con tu esta noche.'

The young lady said, '*Tu* quieres comer con*migo* esta noche?'

'Sí.'

She laughed. So did Lenny. 'Anywhere you like. Take your family too, if it makes you feel better.'

She looked at the other tellers. They gave Lenny a cursory glance and then sniggered behind their painted nails.

'What did I tell you?' said Tarris.

The line behind us had started to make impatient noises. Lenny ignored them. He said to the girl, 'Porque tu no quieres comer con*migo* esta noche?'

The girl got up from her wooden chair, peered over the counter and gave Lenny's outfit the once-over. Then she sat down again. She had thick black hair and large gold hoop earrings.

'Oh,' said Lenny with a smile. 'Fashion snob, huh? My ropas. Is that what the problem is?'

'Eh?'

'No quieres mi ropas, baby?'

'Hor*rible*!' the girl said, making a face. But she was clearly enjoying herself, and so were the other tellers, it was just the customers waiting to do business who weren't.

'All right. That's all right. I've been meaning to do this for some time anyway, and a beautiful girl like you is as good a motive as any. Don't go no place, I'll be right back. Fellas?'

'What?'

'Let's go to market.'

At the top of the hill, behind the bank, was the market. It wasn't a very good market but some stalls offered clothing. Lenny picked his way through the stalls, appraising various items. We followed.

A yellow shirt with a small collar, short sleeves, micro-buttons, made of 100 percent polyester was held up to view. Lenny put it against his chest and grinned.

'Shocking,' said Tarris.

'What do you think?' Lenny asked me.

'It's an improvement on the T-shirt.'

Lenny bought three shirts: the yellow, the purple and the black – all the same model. I bought an army cap with El Salvador written on it. Tarris found an old hippy belt woven with multi-colored threads. Next we went looking for pants. A pair of polyester and cotton slacks, in black, with the correct fitting in the leg and girth, was purchased from a stall nearby.

'Muy elegante,' the stall-owner complimented Lenny.

Muy barato, too. Three bucks.

'Need footwear?' I said, looking down at Lenny's dusty boots with his toes peeking through.

'This way,' said Lenny.

The store was on the corner of two streets with no names. It had glass windows displaying a variety of footwear: sandals, knock-off deck shoes, loafers – some in patent leather and some in fake alligator.

A well-dressed young lady greeted us. Lenny stood at the far end of a rack of shoes, pointing up at a shoe which had caught his eye.

The assistant pulled the box down, took off the top and presented the shoe.

'Beautiful,' said Lenny.

He put it on.

'Whad'ya think?' he asked.

They were standard-issue institution slides; the same shoes they give you in any correctional facility in the United States. Lenny was very taken with them.

'Good ventilation,' he said. 'They're beautiful, huh?'

He strutted up and down the store, holding his wounded arm, gazing at his reflection in the mirror.

'Hellish,' said Tarris, slapping his brown knee and hooting with laughter.

'You like 'em, Tarris?'

But Tarris was laughing too hard to reply.

'Señorita,' said Lenny. 'Estas zapatos? Me gusta mucho. No need to wrap 'em. I'm gonna be wearing 'em right out of here.'

The shoes were paid for. Lenny was now outfitted: new shirt, new pants and now this – a spanking-new pair of institution slippers. At a total cost of about fifteen dollars. He swung the bags jauntily over his shoulder as we walked back through the hot streets to Motel Rick's (Lenny was staying down the street at the plusher Granada, his reasoning being that invalids are entitled to more comforting accommodation than a mattress and a cold shower. The Granada was three-star. The rooms come with balcony, hammock, veranda, bar, restaurant, hot water, an overgrown garden, and something advertised as room service: a sleepy young dude with a nice smile who could make it from the kitchen downstairs to Lenny's room one floor above in about an hour-and-a-half if he was feeling on top of things. Two if he wasn't.)

'Latin chicks,' Lenny said, throwing his bags on the bed. They appreciate a guy who *smells* right, huh? Get me that little wash-bag of yours, Tarris? I need to freshen up.'

Tarris fetched his wash-bag. Lenny held up a variety of airline fragrances in small plastic bottles. They had labels in Russian, Polish, Chinese, Japanese, Indian, Arabic, Hebrew, Italian, English and French – taken from different airlines during Tarris's travels.

'Nuit et Jour,' Lenny said. It had bright white writing in slopey italics. He twisted the cap off and then sniffed the contents.

Lenny disappeared into the bathroom. Fifteen minutes later, now shaved, showered, scrubbed and dressed, he emerged with a towel over his shoulders, holding a can of talcum powder.

'How do I look, gentlemen?'

The hair was slicked back, the shades, a new two-dollar pair, were on; the pants had one crease, not a million, in them; the shirt didn't have any food stains and his prison slides shimmered – you could hardly recognize the man.

'What's so funny?' Lenny asked as he pulled open the waist of his pants and started emptying the talcum powder down his crotch. 'What?'

'Nothing,' I said.

'No. Nothing at all,' said Tarris.

Lenny opened the door and slammed it behind him.

'Bet you a bottle of rum he'll be back in half an hour,' said Tarris.

'Bet you two he won't,' I said.

We didn't see Lenny again. Apparently he had a very good evening with the young lady and her family. And it changed him, too. He threw out his old pants and boots. And he seemed to develop a minor interest in clothes stores. Nothing too excessive. But definitely an interest.

28

At the Honduran Consulate in New York City, the young consul sat me in a chair opposite his desk beneath a flag on the wall and we had a talk. Honduras, he said, was not only one of the most civilized countries in Central and South America, but also a place where I would be welcomed by the local populace. If I was serious about this idiocy of driving to Brazil for carnaval I should exercise great caution when driving through Peru. Peru was full of peasants. Stupid, dangerous, uneducated, they were a mean, wicked bunch. But the Hondurans? They will welcome you with *open* arms!

This was half true. When we pitched up at the Honduran border, the arms were open but so were the palms, and these palms were large and needed large quantities of American dollars to allow access through the country. The hustle the boys had going at the border was flagrant, profitable, and they didn't give a damn if you knew it or not. When I tried presenting my papers, the officials wouldn't take them – not unless I used one of the sanctioned border dogs. The border dogs on the Honduran border were teenagers with $200 Air Jordan hi-tops and American basketball T-shirts. They had nice watches, new jeans, and they wanted a hundred dollars, up front, in exchange for the correct documents to drive for six hours through the countryside to the Nicaraguan frontier. I wasn't paying a hundred bucks to get the paperwork to drive through the country, and I told one of the boys this. He went and snitched to the *Comandante*. The *Comandante* told me that one hundred bucks was what it cost to drive in Honduras. Standard rate. I pointed at my guide-book. It said I had to pay something like six. Not a hundred. The *Comandante* pointed at my car. It's one hundred dollars, he said. Or you have *problemas*. I told him I was paying six and that was all. He got his boys to strip the hearse. Everything came out of the car doors on to the dirt – futon, boogey-boards, empty bottles of mescal, tequila, beer, Tylenol, the coffin – all of it, on the dirt, while the *Comandante* stood with his arms crossed, smiling broadly, very happy with his work.

'Great people-skills, buddy,' Lenny said.

I had to pay the border dog a hundred. But Tarris enjoyed himself thoroughly. The money-changers were as greedy as the *Comandante*. He managed to off-load 700 bucks on them. They didn't care if he had a passport, a fishing license, or a name-tag, they just wanted his business.

'Best border we come through by a long shot,' he said. 'Wish they were all like that. God bless 'em.'

29

Late that afternoon, in the Honduran highlands, Lenny pointed through the glass at a white Cherokee jeep up ahead and said, 'Jesus Christ. That car's got *Ohio* plates. Put your foot down.'

We had not seen a car for hours. Tarris put his foot down. The old hearse coughed. With the altitude, the bad gas, the transmission which had been slipping intermittently since we blew the seal back in Vinton, the performance was down and overtaking was not possible. We followed them for a little while but they turned off at an Esso station.

Lenny said, 'Oh, man, a little *blonde.*'

We pulled into the border station at El Espino shortly after. El Espino was like any other border station in Central America: a series of concrete buildings in a parched hillock setting, with a few soldiers, a barrier, a bridge over a river, another barrier on the other side and a little beverage kiosk selling Chiclets, sodas and beer.

As soon as we pulled in, the money-changers came charging out from their hiding-places shouting, 'AMIGO! AMIGO! DINERO! DINERO! CAMBIAR DINERO AQUI, AMIGO!'

But this time, instead of pulling the undertaking trick with the top hats and the gloves, all we had to do was say those words which work wonders with any businessman in Latin America: 'Rich Americano turista behind, boys. Mucho dinero up the road.'

They shot off up the road to bug the owners of the Cherokee which was a minor disappointment for Tarris. After his great success at the Honduran border six hours earlier he was hoping to get some repeat action on his remaining checks. But the men had run off to seek more profitable pickings.

We started the exit formalities, following the paper trail from one desk to the next inside the customs and immigration hall, helped by about sixteen kids. When we were done we went up to the kiosk where the car was parked and bought beer.

'Hey, you guys! Speak inglés?'

The man was tall, skinny and fresh-faced. His girlfriend was shortish, blonde and pretty. Both wore matching shorts and tops.

I nodded.

'That *your* hearse?'

'It is,' I replied.

'Cool car. Where d'you come from?'

'New York.'

'We came down from Toledo.'

Lenny yawned and made eyes at the young blonde. She looked away.

'My name is Jim. This is Julie, my fiancée. We're engaged to be married.'

We shook hands. Jim asked me our route. I told him. He told me he had entered Honduras from Belize, not Salvador. They were going to Costa Rica. That was their final destination.

'You have problems with the roads?' Jim asked.

'Only finding them.'

'We keep getting flats. But hey — that's okay. We're prepared. Spent four years planning this trip. Got everything you could need. I'm a black belt in karate. Julie here's a nurse. Where you guys going in Nicaragua?'

'Surfin',' said Tarris.

'The beach, huh? That's where we're going!'

'How thrilling,' said Lenny. He got up from his stool and walked off.

'Better be quick with your papers,' I said. 'They shut everything at five. If you don't get it done by then, you won't go anywhere until tomorrow.'

Jim looked at his watch. 'Better hurry, Jool!'

Jim and Julie ran off down the hill to the customs hall.

'Aren't they *cute*?' said Lenny, returning.

'We're going to see them down the beach,' I said.

They didn't get the paperwork finished in time. They needed one more stamp, but the Honduran lady wouldn't give it to them. She shut the office five minutes early. I asked them if they were going to be alright for the night.

'Hey, no problemo,' said Jim. 'We'll put up our tent and cook. We got plenty of food. Don't worry about us, guys.'

We didn't.

30

'Cocktails, gentlemen?' said Lenny.

We were paddling. The hearse was on the beach. It was around eleven the next morning. Lenny had just fixed a fresh batch of his own cocktails, a mix of vodka, mescal and tequila served warm in fresh coconuts with a straw when the Cherokee pulled up on the hot sand and parked next to the hearse.

'Shit,' said Lenny. 'They made it.'

They got out and waved. We waved. Jim whooped and ran down the sand to rush in the water. Julie whooped and ran down after him.

'That little Julie,' said Lenny, 'she sure has a cute bod.'

'How ya doin', guys?' said Jim.

'We're doin' well, thank you, Jim,' I replied. 'Good to see you both made it.'

'What a day!'

'Isn't it?'

'Beautiful. Sure beats winter in the States. Wow, fresh coconuts!' said Jim, pointing at my drink. 'Don't get many fresh coconuts in Toledo at this time of year. You mind?'

He took the coconut from my hand. He started drinking. Then he spat it out.

'*Man*, what *is* that?'

'Potent,' said Lenny, smiling.

'You know, you guys really shouldn't be drinking that stuff in this heat. It can really take it out of you. Jool?'

'What, hon?'

'These guys are *drinking*!'

That day we lay in the sun and swam with Jim and Julie. Lenny was very taken with Julie. When Julie got up to go for a swim, Lenny got up to go for a swim. When Julie wanted a drink, Lenny went off and found her a coconut.

'No funny stuff in it?' she asked.

'Not unless you want some funny stuff.'

'Maybe later.'

But when Julie wanted the coconut opened she went to Jim with his ten-in-one commando knife that he carried in the sheath on his money-belt, along with his phrase-book, his solar-powered pocket calculator, his survival guide-book, his fishing-hook, his monofilament wire, his Spanish dictionary, and a few other key survival tools. Jim was a professional tourist. He had taken Spanish courses, self-defence courses, a mechanics course, read up the history of Central America, and was careful to abide by all the rules for eating, drinking and traveling safely.

'You should meet Susan,' said Lenny.

'Who's Susan?' Jim asked.

'You guys would get on famously. We met her and her friend back in Mexico.'

'Nice people?'

'Lovely.'

Sometime late in the afternoon Lenny discovered that Julie was a runner. He said they should go running together sometime.

'I'd love that, Lenny!' she said. 'Do you run a lot?'

'Just starting, Jool. Going for that buff surfer bod look.'

'I try and run every day. Every day,' said Julie.

'Really?' said Lenny. 'Well, maybe we should go for a little run tomorrow morning.'

'I go early.'

'How does ten sound?'

'Ten? Oh, no! Ten's way too late. In this heat? You'd get sun-stroke. I normally go around six when the sun is just coming up.'

'Jool,' said Jim, who had been listening to this exchange, 'race you in!'

That night we invited Julie and Jim to dine with us in Leon. The restaurant was just off the main square. We'd been there the night before. There were two nice-looking girls who worked behind the bar: Tania and Carolina. We invited Tania and Carolina to come out with us later, if they could just sneak out of the restaurant without their mother catching them. Lenny was still chasing Julie. He sat next to her at dinner. I was at the other end of the table with Tarris, opposite Jim. We had been in there about fifteen minutes when Jim started to worry about Julie's drinking. That was the first thing that bugged him that night.

'You know you can't hold your liquor!' he said. 'So don't drink so fast, Jool!'

'But I like it! It's so sweet,' said Julie.

'Yeah, but it makes you stupid,' said Jim. 'You don't want to act stupid, Jool.'

'Leave the girl alone. For Chrissakes, she's old enough to make her own mind up,' said Lenny, smiling and pouring out more shots of tequila. 'Aren't you, sweetheart?'

'Lenny, this has nothing to do with you.'

'To new friends!' Lenny said, raising his glass.

'To new friends!' said Julie, raising her glass and giggling as it met Lenny's in a salute.

Tarris said, 'D'you think they'd like to go to the casa after this?'

'I thought we weren't going to talk about that in front of them,' I said.

'The casa,' said Tarris. 'That's the place for us.'

'Like another glass there, Jim?' Lenny asked.

'One beer's enough for me, thank you, Lenny.'

'I will!' said Julie.

'Jool? You drink any more, you're going to be sick. Don't give her any more, Lenny.'

Lenny poured her another glass.

'To new friends!' said Lenny.

'And safe traggles!' said Julie.

'*Told* you it would happen,' said Jim. 'I fuckin' told you.'

Later, we found a cab driver, and bought some supplies for

the evening, then went to the Tonel night-club. The Tonel is Leon's premier night-spot. It was dark, loud, hot and crowded. We took a table by the dance-floor, near the video screen which was running a clip on an aerial dogfight.

'Wanna dance, Julie?' Lenny asked.

'Ah –'

'Dance with me,' said Jim.

'Love to,' said Lenny, getting up to dance with Jim. Jim shook off Lenny's hand. 'Not you, moron. I wanna dance with my fiancée.'

Jim and Julie got up to dance.

'Gentlemen,' said Lenny, 'let us adjourn to the toilets.'

In the cubicle, while Tarris was busy racking up the lines, Lenny said, 'That Jim. He really plays damned good defence.'

Back in the club, the music was salsa, then musica romantica. Jim and Jool danced neatly in one corner. We tried our hand with the ladies. Nothing cooking. Girls danced with girls, or with their boyfriends, but not gringos. And no one wanted their palms read, either.

'That's it,' said Tarris, returning to the table. 'Let's go.'

'Where d'you wanna go, Tarris?' Jim asked.

'The casa. This place is doing my fucking nut.'

'Another club?' said Jim. 'Cool.'

A large, sweating young man wearing a blazer, shirt and tie came up to the table to ask Julie for a dance.

'Hey!' said Jim. 'What's going on here?'

'He's asking for a dance,' I said.

'Just wait a minute, pal,' said Jim. 'Julie, d'you want me –'

'Relax,' said Tarris. 'Nothing's going to happen.'

'Julie?'

'What?'

'Shall I tell this –?'

But Julie was up from her seat and heading for the dance-floor with the young Nicaraguan. Jim started doing his kung fu warm-up routine under the table.

Lenny said, 'Whad'ya think he's going to do? *Rape* her?'

'This is Nicaragua, Lenny. Nicaragua is dangerous. Our government has been waging war down here for –'

Julie came back to the table.

'Have fun, Julie?' Lenny asked.

'This guy is really a *great* dancer,' said Julie, pointing at the heavy-set young Nicaraguan.

'Martín,' said the young man, wiping his brow with his handkerchief and then holding out his hand.

'Would you like to join us, Martín?' I asked.

Martín had extremely good manners and he came to the table with a full bottle of rum.

'I'll take a glass,' I said. 'Thank you.'

'And me!' said Julie.

'That's my girl,' said Lenny, offering his glass.

'What did you say, Lenny?' asked Jim.

'Jim?' I said.

'What?'

'Would you give me a hand fixing the exhaust before we leave?'

'Huh?'

'I broke a bracket last night on the way into town. You seem to be a practical man, would you help me fix it before we leave?'

Jim followed me out to the street where I'd paid a kid a dollar to watch the car. Jim crawled under the car and fixed the bracket. I watched and smoked.

'That ought to do it,' he said.

'Kind of you,' I said.

'Hey, no problem. But tell me something. Is that friend of yours always such an asshole?'

We went back inside. Martín and Julie were dancing. When they returned, I said, 'Martín, you want to come with us?'

'Dónde vas?'

'What's that place called?' I asked.

'The Restaurante Primavera,' said Tarris.

'The Restaurante Primavera,' I said.

'Ai! Ai! Ai!' said Martín. 'Esta es una casa de putas, no?'

'What's he saying?' asked Jim.

'Sí,' I replied.

'Es muy peligroso, hombre!' said Martín. 'Muy, muy peligroso.'

'I don't understand,' said Jim. 'What's muy peligroso?'

'Restaurante Primavera,' said Martín.

'What's the Restaurante Primavera?'

'Una casa de putas,' said Martín.

'What's a casa de pootas?'

'A whore-house, Jim,' said Lenny. 'Woops, I shouldn't have *said* that.'

Jim blanched. 'Jool. The guys wanna go to a *whore*-house!'

'I think it'd be kinda interesting.'

'What did you say?'

'I said it'd be kinda interesting.'

'They want to go to a *whore*-house! Not a *night*-club.'

'I know.'

Jim shrugged. 'You wait till we get home. Your mother will fuckin' freak.'

'Only if you tell her.'

The Restaurante Primavera was on the far side of the main square. It was a large open bar with wood tables, entertainment suites in the back, and a sound system that played 'Knights in White Satin' on a perpetual loop. Lucy was hostess. We'd been there the night before. She got so drunk she threw up.

Lucy was a large, friendly, inebriated lady wearing a pair of stone-washed jeans size thirty-eight and a 40-D brassière. She came over to welcome us back.

Then she saw Jim.

And he did something to her. She could not take her eyes off him. I think it was his blond hair.

'Hola . . . guapo!' she said, grabbing him and kissing him.

Jim pulled away from her and laughed nervously.

'I don't *think* so, señora!'

'Señorita, señor!' Lucy corrected.

'That's Lucy,' I said. 'She's the hostess here.'

'Pleased to meet you, Lucy,' said Jim, holding out his hand.

'Fucky-sucky?' she asked.

'What did she say?' Jim asked.

'Don't ask,' I said.

'Quieres fucky-sucky, hombre?'

'Oh, man!' said Jim. 'That's so gross!'

Lucy walked off laughing.

The room was crowded with groups of young Nicaraguan men. Tarris started palm-reading. We took a table. Lucy came over to sit at our table and made a spot for herself next to Jim. Jim kept asking me when were we thinking of leaving.

'Soon.'

'Bailar, Jeem?' Lucy asked.

'No, gracias,' said Jim.

'Por favor?'

'No. Go dance with someone else. I'm engaged to be married.'

Lucy wasn't listening. She stroked his hair. 'Que bello!' she cooed.

'Thank you.'

'De la botella?'

'No. This is natural.'

'Como este,' said Lucy plucking a handful of her orange hair. 'Natural de la botella!'

'What a freak,' said Jim.

Lucy's cheeks suddenly filled, her eyes ballooned and her face drained of color.

'Oh boy,' I said.

'Here we go,' said Tarris.

'Not again,' said Lenny, moving his chair back.

'What's the matter?' Jim asked.

Lucy vomited. All over the floor. Like she did the night before. It was the third time in two nights we had watched people vomit at the table. It seemed to be a local custom at the weekend. Lucy reached for Jim's beer to wash the taste away.

'That's it!' said Jim. 'That is fucking *it*! I'm going to the car! Jool? Are you coming with me?'

'No,' said Julie. 'I think I'll join you in a minute.'

'Julie, did you hear me? I said I'm going to the goddamn car.'

'So go.'

I gave Jim the keys. Jim marched out of the bar on to the street. Fifteen minutes later, he marched back.

'Where's Julie?' he asked.

'In the bathroom,' I said.

'Where's Lenny?' he asked.

Julie and Lenny came back through the restaurant, laughing. Lenny had his arm around Julie's shoulder. Tarris was off at another table – earlier some shy young men had come to our table to ask me to ask Tarris if he would consider introducing them to the ladies, since with his palmistry talents he seemed to be the most popular man in the house.

'Julie, I'd like to speak to you outside,' said Jim.

'Alrighty.'

'Don't be long now, Julie,' said Lenny. Julie laughed. Jim led Julie outside. Lenny sat down next to me.

'She really is a nice kid,' Lenny said. 'But what the hell is she doing with that dolt?'

Jim came back to the table.

'We're going to wait in the car,' he said. 'How long are you guys going to be?'

'Not long,' I said.

Two hours later Jim was pretty angry.

'This is *not* fair,' he said. 'We wanna go home.'

'Won't be long.'

'We want to go now!'

I went to get Tarris. Tarris wasn't ready to leave.

'They have to go home and make their tent,' I explained.

'Tell 'em to come back inside and have a drink.'

'They don't want to come back inside and have a drink. They want to go to bed.'

'They can go to bed in the car.'

'They don't want to go to bed in the car. They want to go to bed in their tent.'

'I thought they wanted to come out for the night.'

'They did.'

Tarris was having a good evening with his new friends on the local American football team. There was about five empty liter bottles of rum on their table. 'Tell 'em to fuck off, then.'

I drove them back down to the beach with Lenny. It was a

forty-minute drive. The kids didn't speak to us all the way there. At the Cherokee, they got out. In the beams from our headlamps we watched Jim trudge over the sand, leading Julie by the hand. They were having an argument about something. An hour later we were back in town to pick up Tarris. We arrived as the club was closing. Tarris was outside, circling a spot on the pavement like an old hound about to make his bed for the night. He was with his new friends. They were all looped. Lucy was with them too.

'Boys!' Tarris called. 'I thought you'd buggered off and left me!'

'We had,' I said.

'But we're back. Now get in the car. We had to make a two-hour round trip because of you. Get in and shut up,' said Lenny.

'Boys!' said Tarris, gleefully. 'You came back! You came back for ol' Tarris!'

I opened the door and herded the old drunk on to the seat.

'You're a disgrace,' I told him.

Tarris collapsed on the front seat and giggled. Then he got all sentimental about the powers of friendship.

'This is when you know you got good friends,' he said. 'When they'll drive through the night to come pick you up.'

The drunk young Nicaraguans raised their bottles. 'Luego, Tarris!'

'Aaar!'

Lucy stepped up to the car window. She leaned inside and asked me where the *guapo* was.

'Here, my darlin',' said Tarris, giving her a lascivious wink.

'No, no, no! Quiero Jim!' she exclaimed.

'Jim es a la playa,' I told her.

'Yo lo quiero!' she uttered.

Lucy had the hots for little Jimmy. The only fair thing to do in this situation was to pop Lucy in the back and take her back down to the beach with us.

So we did.

31

The tent had been set up on the sand, just down the beach from the palm trees where we had the hammocks strung.

'Now, Luce,' I said as we stood next to the hearse. It was cold but the sun was just coming up. 'In that tent over there Señor Jim is fast asleep.'

'Qué?'

Lenny translated.

'But Señor Jim told me he liked you very much.'

Lenny translated.

'But here's the problem. The girlfriend.'

Lucy got it.

'La gringa?'

'Yes. This is what we should do –'

'I'm liking every goddamn minute of this,' said Lenny. 'Where's my running shoes?'

Lucy tipped the bottle of tequila up and drank off about a third of it. Tarris adjusted his Angels baseball cap while Lenny lit a cigarette.

'What do we do if he starts going crazy with that kung-fu shit?'

'Run.'

'Who's going to go wake him up?' asked Tarris.

'You,' I said.

'Why me?'

'Because you were the bastard we had to drive two hours' round trip to pick up. Anyway, he thinks you're the most grown-up around here.'

'That's right,' said Lenny. 'He does. He told me.'

Tarris grunted and picked up a flashlight. He walked over the cold sand towards the sea and their tent. I rolled under the hearse. Lucy got in the hearse. Lenny went off to hide in the coconut grove. A few minutes later I saw a light go on in the tent. Then I saw the black silhouette of Jim sit up and start to dress. Jim and Tarris came walking back across the sand.

'What are his symptoms?' I heard Jim ask.

'Well, lemme see now. He looks terrible,' Tarris said. 'And his voice –'

'His *voice*?'

'A little higher.'

'You guys aren't taking malaria pills, are you?'

'Can't remember.'

I heard the back door open.

'It's alright, fella. Help is at hand,' said Jim. 'Now, let's see you.'

'Hola!' said Lucy, on cue.

'Oh God! It's *you*!'

Jim and Julie didn't stay to enjoy the beautiful sunrise. They split. We had a few more cocktails, then retired to the hammocks. Lucy slept in the back of the hearse. In the morning we all went for a swim and then had breakfast. We drove Lucy back to Leon and sometime after lunch we headed out for Managua to try to get the exhaust patched.

32

A couple of days later, with patches on the exhaust and new brackets fixed for us at a little shack on the outskirts of Managua (the mechanic's assistant was a little goat called Eric. Eric snacked on exhaust pipes), we were on route to Costa Rica, driving Nicaragua's main highway, the Nica 2, along the volcanic shoreline of the Lago, past the sleeping volcanoes. It was getting late in the afternoon, it had been hot, we had not been able to find ice for our bowls, and we needed refreshing, when the notion of a little detour off the highway down to the warm Pacific to freshen up with a swim, a plate of shrimp and some cold beer was mooted.

'Cracking idea,' said Tarris. 'Watch the sun go down, a bite to eat and a beer. Perfecto.'

That was the plan. But something else postponed it and his name was Carlos Greene. Carlos Greene was a fisherman. We met him while sitting at the only bar in the little fishing village of Porto Astoria watching the sun sink out in the bay. He walked in and asked who owned the big *puta madre de carroza* parked outside at the curb.

'That would be me,' I said.

Carlos loved the hearse. He wanted to know if it was really a Cadillac, if it was a V8, how many liters, how fast, what kind of gas mileage – all of that. He spoke English and Spanish. He introduced himself as a shrimp-boat captain. We introduced ourselves. He eyed the bottle of rum on the table. We invited him to join us. Carlos was a small man, weathered, about fifty. He pulled out a chair and sat.

'Un otro vaso, por favor,' I asked the proprietress.

When the glass was brought to the table Carlos filled it with ice from the glass bowl, poured rum over the ice and then squeezed a lime over it and stirred it with his finger. Lenny padded out to the car in his slides to fetch the bug spray. Carlos said the company he worked for was a big fishing fleet which owned the three barges out in the bay and the five shrimp boats. Now it's called Sandapesce. Once it was called Nicasur.

'They are clever,' said Carlos. 'They change the name of the company with every government to make the government happy. Now they are for Sandinista. Before they were for Somoza.'

'Carlos,' said Tarris, 'where are the women in this town?'

'They are at home,' said Carlos.

'I have heard it said that Nicaraguan women are the most beautiful in Central America.'

'They are,' said Carlos. 'But they are at home.'

'What are you doing for dinner?'

'No sé.'

'Perhaps you might like to join us and invite some young ladies too?'

And that's where it all started.

A little after sunset Carlos returned. The village was now in complete darkness. There was a power cut. The proprietor of the bar put some candles on our table along with a mosquito coil.

'It is very bad,' Carlos said, shaking his head and batting at a mosquito.

'What is very bad?' I asked.

'This. Now the girls will not come. I tell them about you. They are curious. They want to come for dinner, but now? Tsk! They will not.'

'Why not?'

'They are frightened of rape. In my village it happens

often. A jealous man who has seen a woman around the town. The woman say to him no. He waits. When there is no power he hides. When she is walking solo – it happens many time in Porto Astoria. Now the women will never come. But in the town of Corinto –' he made the gesture as if he had burnt his fingers – 'incredible! The most *beautiful* girls. In all Nicaragua.'

'No shit, Carlos,' said Lenny.

'Whoop, whoop,' said Tarris. 'Where is this town Corinto?'

'The other side of Leon.'

'How long a drive?'

'In a car like un Caddy-yac? Three hours. No más.'

Tarris looked at me, then at Lenny. 'As Secretary of Enterta —'

'I know what you're going to say,' I said. 'And the answer is no.' I'd settled on the idea of a peaceful night tucked up in the hearse at the frontier, a good eight hours of rest, ready for Costa Rica and San José.

'Why, bunje?'

'Because it's too far. And for what?'

'Pussy,' said Tarris, with a grin.

'How many hours to Corinto?' I asked.

'Only two, two-and-a-half,' said Carlos.

And like idiots we believed him.

We bought a bottle of rum and some beer from the restaurant. When we stopped to fill with gas, we grinned at the Indian farmers sitting in the back of an old Japanese pick-up who stared at the big black hearse sitting at the pump island. Half a bottle of rum later, we ran through a military checkpoint.

'Stop!' shouted Carlos, banging his hand on the dash.

'Why?'

'You must! Or they *kill* us!'

I hit the brakes. Carlos pointed at the angry guards standing in the road beckoning for us to reverse. We turned the music off. We hid the rum. When the soldiers saw what kind of car was slowly approaching them in something resembling a straight line they shooed us on our way.

One hour and forty minutes later we came down a narrow, twisting hill road to a town of lights, the first lights for a long time. Off in the distance was a much larger glow of dull yellow sulphurous light against the night sky.

'Managua?' I asked.

'Leon,' said Carlos emphatically.

'Looks like Managua to me,' I said.

'You do not know!' said Carlos. 'I know this road! I am ship's pilot! I know the way! It is where we must go – Leon. But first we look for the *short road*!'

'Exactly,' Lenny giggled. 'The short road, man.'

A little further: '*Here!*'

Carlos pointed proudly at a sandy track that veered off perpendicularly from the road.

'You sure about this, Carlos?' I asked.

'Claro, hombre! Directo!'

I cranked the wheel. We bumped on to the rutted track. It was sand and dirt, not leveled. But they were working on it. The hearse ploughed through these sand tracks, the nose bouncing up and down, raising great clouds of dust. After twenty minutes of it I got in the swing of things. We hurtled down this sand track, disappearing in and out of gullies. Now and then there would be signs pointing to a detour through an area. The deviation would dip down a long sandy gully. The trick was to use these as slingshots. If you set it up right you could launch Tarris three to three-and-a-half feet in the air.

One hour passed. Then another. I started to get bored. Tarris got bruised. Carlos got drunk. Then he fell asleep. Just before passing out he said, 'Maybe this is not the right road.'

Around midnight, miles from anywhere, we came to a military checkpoint. A soldier in a green uniform stood waving a torch. Ahead a bus was already stopped and an inspection underway. I pulled over.

'What do you think they want?' Lenny asked.

'Papers. Wake Tarris up.'

'Tarris?' said Lenny.

'What?'

'Checkpoint.'

Bags came flying off the roof of the bus. They also came through the bus windows.

'Where are we?' Tarris asked.

'Near Corinto,' said Carlos.

Tarris muttered something. In the rear-view I watched him throw off the blanket and look for his shoes and baseball cap. An army man and his young sidekick with jackboots and rifle slung over a shoulder came back to the window and shone a light in my face.

'Documentación!'

I fished around in my strongbox, then handed over the title, my international driver's license and my passport. All the booze had been hidden. They studied the passports.

'Dame un cigarrillo!' the soldier instructed.

I gave him a cigarette. I lit it for him. In his right hand he held a copy of *Playboy* magazine which he had just confiscated from a passenger on the bus.

'Problema!' the guard said.

'Por qué?' I asked.

The man jabbed his chubby finger at the stamps in my passport. Then he started talking away fast and irate and I didn't follow a word of it. Carlos, who had sobered instantly, listened and then translated. The little stamps in my passport were not in order. The car ought to have been out of Nicaragua five o'clock that afternoon.

'Impossible,' I said.

'A las cinco!' the man shouted.

Thing to do in these situations is lie.

'Ah, escuchame, Capitán,' I said. 'Yo give mucho dinero a el Comandante a la frontera. Comprendes? Mucho dinero to the Comandante para ir en tránsito para *treinte* dias! No *seis* dias. *Treinte* dias!'

I was telling him I'd spent a lot of money buying a thirty-day pass from the *Comandante*. I hadn't, but it's better to start high and bargain down.

He let off another stream of fast, angry Spanish.

'Guy says you an illegal,' said Carlos. 'He says you have a big problema, hombre. Says you can go to jail.'

Tarris started snickering.

'He can't mean that,' I said.

'You don't understand, amigo. You have no power here. They do what they want.'

'What's he want me to do?'

'Go with him to the hut.'

'This is not good,' said Lenny.

I started to consider a night or two in the Nicaraguan clink. So did Tarris. In light of what had happened to him over the last couple of hours, being slung against the roof of the hearse, this perked him up considerably.

'I'll come with you, bunje,' said Tarris. 'Find out where they're gonna take you.'

We got out. Over the buzz of cicadas we heard laughter from the bus – the driver and the young soldier were studying the *Playboy* magazine by flashlight. They concluded that white chicks have bigger breasts than Nicaraguan chicks. And less hair, which is not so sexy.

The officer turned to Carlos. 'What are you doing with *them?*' He pointed a disparaging finger at me who was having a smoke and Tarris who was urinating in the scrub at the margin of the road.

Carlos told the officer he was a captain from the village of Porto Astoria in the south; that he was traveling with us because we were potential investors in a fishing vessel. That is why we were all going to the great port of Corinto. To inspect a fishing boat. At one in the morning.

'If they are businessmen,' the soldier said craftily, 'why are they traveling in a car for the dead?'

'Because they are loco.'

'Come!'

'I'll watch the car,' said Lenny.

The bus, now repacked with bags and passengers, released the air-brakes and pulled away from the hard-shoulder in a cloud of black smoke.

We were led up a hillock path to a hut at the top. Inside it was small, candle-lit, and smelled of oiled gun metal. Rifles were stacked neatly against the wall, butt-to-floor, barrel-to-wall. The *Comandante* sat at a desk that took up most of the hut. He was a whale of a man in a green tunic with a green cap and a mustache. My papers were shown. He shook his head.

'Es un problema,' he told me, which wasn't any great

surprise. Then he said something about me being illegal and what a serious offense this was.

I lied a little more. I told him I was made to pay fifty dollars to enter . . .

'Cincuenta dollares?' the *Comandante* exclaimed.

Yes, I told him. And I had paid this sum and paid it gladly, in full, looking forward to my travels in this great country . . .

'En una *carroza*?' the *Comandante* interrupted.

'Yes,' I replied proudly. 'Pero en paz, Comandante. Y ahora, yo, un inocente, tengo un gran problema y es possible que yo puedo ir a –' and here I couldn't remember the phrase for going to jail.

'Cárcel,' said Tarris, helpfully.

'Thank you, Tarris. Cárcel,' I said. 'Y por qué?'

I was surprised by my sudden fluency with the Spanish language, but jail will do that. The *Comandante* wanted to know what border we crossed.

I told him again.

'No es possible!' he said, shaking his head. 'Mi *hermano* es el capitán allá!'

Well, I thought. That's blown that little idea. If his brother is the border captain and I've just accused him of being a venal, corrupt little bastard, I could only expect the worst. But luckily there was some bad blood between the *Comandante* here and his younger brother. The *Comandante* asked me if I had a receipt. I said he wouldn't give me a receipt. The *Comandante* was not surprised. He even apologized to me. The *Comandante* was the first straight soldier we'd met.

'You,' Tarris whispered in a tone that suggested great disappointment, 'are a lucky bastard.'

That night I learned that corruption was a terrible disease in Nicaragua. But the country was young with democracy.

Progress was coming. One day Nicaragua would be a country which people from all over the world would want to visit . . .

'I can see that.'

However, change does not come overnight. And these papers of mine were not in order. But if we were to go straight to the border station of Peñas Blancas that evening, I would not be arrested.

'The Comandante is a great man,' I said. 'Where is the road for Peñas Blancas?'

'Directo!' he replied, like everybody always did.

He gave me a piece of paper authorizing me to drive on the roads of Nicaragua until eight o'clock the following morning. We turned to leave.

The *Comandante* had one final word of advice. In Spanish he said something like, 'Do not pay that fat pig of a customs man. He is greedy and will try to keep you here. Do not pay him a single córdoba!'

'It will be my pleasure,' I replied.

We made the border station by about five after dropping Carlos home. The border station with Costa Rica was deluxe by comparison with all the others. They have a bar there with a man in a bow-tie and white shirt selling German beer at nine in the morning. And fresh coffee. The first fresh coffee we'd had in Central America.

33

'So you guys really drove *all* the way here from New York?' an American in the lounge of the Casita Inn, San Jose, asked us. It was now five in the evening.

'That's right.'

A German photographer we'd met while being fleeced at the border of Honduras and El Salvador had recommended the Casita Inn to us as a pleasant, reasonable place to stay.

'That's incredible,' said the American. 'And how was it, guys? You have any trouble?'

'No.'

'*No?*'

The owner of the inn recommended we visit the Pueblo district as newcomers to San Jose. The Pueblo district, she assured us, had great character. After showering we went to the Pueblo district. What a tip. Heaps of bars and restaurants and jewelry stores and tourist groups saying things like, 'Marvin, doesn't this remind you of the Imperial Market in Honolulu?'

We didn't stop for a beer in the Pueblo district.

An hour later we were standing in the men's room of the Holiday Inn admiring the facilities.

'Boy,' said Lenny as we stood looking at the clean, tiled, empty cubicles with toilets, soft toilet paper, seats and muzak, 'if only I had to go, man. I have been dreaming of toilets like these for *weeks*.'

We took three cubicles. For ten minutes we sat there and it was most pleasant. We slid a pack of Marlboros from one cubicle to the next, and discussed what to do for the rest of the evening.

On the street, we walked down the long line of cabbies parked outside the Holiday Inn. A cab-driver called Oscar took us crosstown to the Happy Days, Happier Nights bar. We were assigned three young ladies as soon as we walked in: Flossie, Maria and Monica. They wanted to go dancing next door at the Key Largo night-club.

Inside the Key Largo, Flossie said she had a terrible

headache, did not want to dance, she needed a big drink. Flossie's best friend was a woman called Carro. Carro was about fifty, had five grandchildren and an enormous appetite. I bought Carro three sandwiches. When the place closed a couple of hours later, the girls said, 'Where we go now?'

'We were thinking of the hotel.'

'We come with you!'

'Good.'

'How we get there?'

'By car.'

They liked this idea. Until we got round the corner and I pointed to the hearse.

'Una carroza?'

'No,' said Tarris. 'Una *limousina.*'

'Para los muertos?' the girls asked.

'Por las chicas!' he said.

It took some explaining. Tourists in hearses are not a combo regularly encountered. The girls had a little conference.

'We come with you,' said Flossie. 'If it is near.'

Back at the Casita guest-house, room service had finished. There was no bar and no lounge to sit in, so we went to Lenny's room. Lenny always had a couple of bottles of rum or tequila in his bag. It turned into a little party. Flossie whispered in my ear that she wanted a hundred bucks.

'Why?' I asked.

'Fucky-sucky?'

I thanked her for her offer and declined. Flossie was insulted. She said something to her friend. Lenny said, 'Kids? Why don't you continue this conversation in the privacy of *your* room? Monica and me are going to do some drawing.'

I led Flossie across the hall.

'Would you like me to take you home?' I asked.

'I do not want to go home! I want to stay with you!'

'Okay.'

'For one hundred dollars.'

'I'd better take you home.'

'No! She will kill me! *Kill* me!'

'Who?'

'Carro.'

I opened the door and we went inside.

'Why?'

'For leaving with you. She will be waiting.'

'I bought her three sandwiches and a hot dog. We're good friends.'

'Not with me.'

Flossie was distressed.

'I'd better take you home.'

'*No!* I want to stay with you!'

'Okay.'

'For one hundred dollars!'

I had two beds in my room.

'You take that bed,' I said. 'I'll sleep over here.'

Flossie sat on one bed. I sat on the other. Then I turned the lights off. I was tired. Flossie came over to the bed and leaned over me.

'You no like me?' she asked.

'I like you very much, Flossie.'

'Then you sleep with me!'

'Okay.'

'For one hundred dollars!'

'No.'

'I am worth it!'

'I know you are. But where I come from this is not a good thing to do unless you're a movie star.'

'Why?'

'I can't explain it in Spanish.'

I rolled over. Flossie balled up her fist and hit me on the shoulder.

'What?' I asked.

'Am I not pretty?'

'You are very pretty.'

'Then make love with me!'

'Okay.'

'For one hundred dollars!'

We played this game for about an hour. We started at a hundred, we got down to five and a couple of new dresses and we even laughed about it, too. In the morning the lady who ran the inn said, 'You are *not* allowed to bring those –' and her voice quivered.

'Why?'

'You must leave and you must pay *extra*! For those –'

The bell-boy in the place thought this was first-class entertainment. He sniggered behind his hand as we paid the extra surcharges, took the ladies home, made dates for the evening, then moved downtown to a spot where the atmosphere was a little more relaxed. Hotel called El Dorrado. It had no running water, no electricity, but it was only three bucks a night. Tarris, on principle, still found this sum exorbitant, and we had to meet him halfway down the street when we checked out of there a day later, the manager waiting for him to come down the stairs and pay.

'You are incredible,' said Lenny.

'No running water,' said Tarris. 'Shitter blocked up. Lie on the bed and the thing starts moving – it's worse than an Antiguan jail. Man should be ashamed of himself.'

34

Here was the scene on the ninth floor of the Vera Cruz Hotel in downtown Panama City a few days later: there was a gun-fight going on downstairs in the street, Lenny was flicking through the escort pages of the local yellow pages, I was watching Southern Command TV and Tarris was making lines of some pretty good Panamanian flake cocaine in the toilet.

Anthony was our cab connection. We were walking down the Avenida Peru with Sebastien, a merchant seaman from the Bronx, whose ship had been seized by customs for running guns to Salvador, when Anthony leaned out of his cab window and said, 'Hey, buddies, you needa hotel?'

We started talking. Anthony said it was his business to provide the tourists with whatever they wanted, and as we needed a lot — a good garage to get the hearse serviced, a shipper to get it shipped down into Colombia, a nice hotel with a twenty-four-hour coffee shop, room service, swimming-pool, mini-bar and a few other goods and services — and we needed it quick, we hired him. He took us to the Vera Cruz.

Now he was here to pick us up and show us the town. The first place he thought we'd like to go was called My Place. My Place was a GI bar with two MPs on the door, tin hats, guns, big boots and a bar full of servicemen in tropical beach shirts and shorts, watching videos on the video juke-box. We stayed in My Place two minutes.

'Not what we want,' we told Anthony when we walked out.

'You want to go to night-club?'

'Yes. A *nice* night-club, Anthony.'

Anthony took us to the Bikini Club. Tarris read palms.

Lenny drew sketches of the five girls assigned to our table. Anthony told me about his great marriage. His wife was an Indian. They had three children. He had another child with his mistress. He didn't talk to his mistress any more, but he bought clothes and school supplies and picked the kid up every day after school and took him to McDonald's. Anthony said he had learned his lesson. 'When I want a woman, I come here. Clean! See doctor three times one week! I finish. Thirty dollars. I go home. Is nice. No problems.'

'Where did you learn English?'

'I am taxi-driver. I must know *everything* in Panama! I speak Japan, Italiano, English. But Japan tourist best. Big tippers! Think nothing to give me three-hundred-dollar gold Ronson lighter if they have nice time. Tomorrow, you need car fix, buddy?'

'Full service. And I need some tie-rod bushings to fix the front end. And a new hub cap. And a shine, Anthony. And when that's finished I want to go visit a shipping agent to arrange getting the car down into Colombia.'

'We have very busy day,' said Anthony happily.

35

When Anthony saw the hearse parked in the hotel parking lot he said, 'My buddy's got a *carroza*!'

I told him the car was first priority of business for the day.

'You follow me,' he said. 'We get good service. My buddy best mechanic in Panama!'

I followed Anthony out of the parking lot and we drove down the hill to the seafront, ten minutes away. It was a hot day with a good breeze coming off the bay. We drove along the front in the morning traffic. Some people were walking on the sidewalk near the sea-wall. A few container ships were off on the horizon heading out from the canal into the flat blue Pacific.

The garage was just off Avenida Sur. Anthony parked on the street and beckoned for me to take the car into the lot where five Japanese cars were waiting in front of three open garages with lifters and grease-guns and work-benches and trolleys of tools with mechanics bent over the cars in oily overalls. It was as well stocked and as professional as any operation at any garage in North America. I was glad Anthony had brought me here.

He introduced me as his best buddy. He said what he'd arranged with the owner was for the man to give me a very good price for all the work and he'd have it finished by five that afternoon. That's what he said he said. What he probably told him was, 'This idiot doesn't know a socket set from a torque wrench, you fix up any price you want – but not too high. Give me fifteen percent for bringing him to you, and we got a deal.'

'Cien dollares!' the garage owner quoted gleefully.

'*What?*' I asked.

'For everything, buddy!' said Anthony, grinning.

'A hundred bucks for an oil and filter change?'

'Panama not cheap, buddy! Since the invasion! American soldiers drive price high.'

'He wants more money than I'd be charged in America, Anthony. And I'm supplying the motor oil, the transmission fluid, the fuel, oil and air-filters and –'

'Yes, yes, but big job, buddy! The work for all day! Mercedes in Panama is four hundred dollar for service! Suspension big job! Tune-up and timing much work! Good price, buddy. Very good price. Now we go buy bushing! I know where! Tony know!'

With about four weeks to get to Brazil I wanted to get the car fixed and tuned by the end of the day. Then it could be loaded on the ferry and we could be in Cartagena, Colombia, in two days. The service here in Panama City was an important one. There wouldn't be another place for parts until, I imagined, Lima, Peru. It was worth paying the extra money if the job would be done properly. I took out all the spares purchased in Laredo which were stored down in the compartment underneath the floor in the back, laid them out in the front seat, left the keys in the ignition and went off with Anthony to find the *auto repuestos* shop.

The bushing from the store didn't fit. We went back to the store twice. This took all morning. I bought Anthony lunch. In the afternoon we went to the shipper Anthony knew. We arrived at a modern building in the Miraflores district, took an elevator up to the fourth floor, and walked into the reception area where the secretary took one look at Anthony, fingered him for a cabby, and said haughtily, 'Qué?'

Anthony explained my business. She told us to wait. Soon a young man in a pressed shirt and pants, tie, and patent leather loafers with a lot of toe-cleavage came through a door. He asked me to follow him and led me through to his office. Anthony waited outside.

The shipper's offices were much better furnished than I had expected for a simple ferry outfit. The whole floor was open-plan offices with carpets and glass and stainless steel and plush sofas and even copies of *Hola!* magazine on some tables. Up on the walls were pictures of container ships. I didn't see any car ferries.

The young man asked me to take a seat.

'Where do you want to go?' he asked. His English was very good.

'Cartagena.'

'When?'

'Tomorrow.'

He nodded his head.

'What do you want to send?'

'My car.'

'How long is the car?'

'Twenty-one feet.'

'That's problem.'

'Why?'

'Containers come in twenty and forty feet. You will need a forty.'

'I don't want to send the car by container. I want it to go on a ferry. Roll-on, roll-off. I want to travel with it.'

'No possible.'

'Why not?'

'We don't take passengers. Nobody take passengers.'

'So how much would you charge to ship my car?'

'Three thousand dollars.'

'For a six-hour *ferry* ride?'

'It is the price.'

I had planned on a couple of hundred. As a matter of interest I asked him when his first container boat was going.

'I have one going in two weeks from Colon. You will have to fly to Cartagena and pick it up.'

I asked if they had a boat going to Buenaventura any earlier. Buenaventura was over on the Pacific coast.

'Ten days,' he said.

'Is this also a container?'

'Yes.'

'Same price?'

'A little less.'

'And are all the boats going into Colombia containers?'

'No. Some are roll-on, roll-off.'

'I want to go tomorrow.'

'You will have to try another agent.'

I asked him who. He wasn't about to give business to a competitor. On the way out of reception I lifted a shipping paper from the table. There were advertisements for every shipping agent in Panama City.

Anthony was waiting outside the office, down the hall by the elevator. He wanted to know what happened. I told him the man wanted $3000 to put the car in a container and I didn't want to put the car in a container.

'Is no problem for my buddy. I have friend who is a captain in Colon. He will know about shipping. I ask him.'

The car was ready when we got back to the garage just before five. The owner proudly showed me the oil-can empties to prove he had used my oil – though why he assumed I would think the oil had gone in my car and not one of his seemed strange. The heat, the noise, the news about the container boats and the frustration had given me a headache.

'You want car-wash now, buddy?' said Anthony, whose enthusiasm about anything that he could put ten percent on was endless.

'How much?'

'Five dollars. Good price.'

We went up one block from the garage and parked opposite a lawyer's office. This was the best car-wash in Panama: Three barefoot street kids with buckets, sponges, soap and a dustpan and brush set to work. Anthony talked to them. They talked money but I was too tired to listen. When they started working, Anthony came over.

'You have cigarette for Tony?'

I gave him a cigarette.

'You see that office there? Is the office of a lawyer. Assassinated last week. Colombians come into his office and shoot him five times in the head. Walk out. Never catch them. Nobody see nothing. Muchos traficantes here in Panama. And narco police. Two narco come to me. They say, "Tony, you can buy some coke?" But Tony smart. Tony know they are from narco because they are big gringo men and they want kilo. So I say I cannot get them kilo and they say, "Tony, we make you *rich* man. Very rich man. You never have to work again!" I say I don't want to be rich! I have taxi. I make good money! Nine hundred dollars a month! Narco find greedy bell-boy. Bell-boy in hotel say he know where to buy kilo for narco. Now bell-boy have eight year in cárcel.'

The hearse was finished.

'Look! Good job, buddy!'

I gave him five dollars.

'No, buddy,' said Anthony. 'Is twenty!'

'You told me five, Anthony.'

'For wash. But for wash, clean and hoover? And very quick? Is twenty! Good price, buddy.'

36

The active ingredient in Mace is Phenylchloromethylketone (CN). The instructions are explicit and very helpful: 'Use with care with intoxicated, drugged, demented, enraged or other persons having reduced sensitivity to pain. Remember: aim, spray, walk away!'

That means, instead of blasting the assailant with a one-second burst you douse the bastard with a six-second blast. Colon was the only place in Central America where Mace felt as comforting as sun-block. The following day we went up to Colon to visit the shipping offices of Wilford and McKay. Over the phone the agent told me they had a boat going to Cartagena. They said we'd have to go up to the offices in Colon to pay, finalize the paperwork and meet the customs agent who would broker the deal at the port.

Anthony had told me a funny story about Colon. Prior to the American invasion, the CIA came down and armed the rebels, thinking that when the US troops arrived they'd join forces and point the guns at Noriega. It didn't turn out that way. The rebels turned them on the US troops, then kept the guns when it was all over. Now they used them to stick up tourists.

On the second floor of one of the few buildings that wasn't falling down (Colon was the Caribbean version of a dilapidated New Orleans) was the shipping office. It was a room full of desks with blacks or Indians either on the phone or sitting behind old typewriters. I asked if anybody spoke English. Nobody spoke English. In fact nobody spoke anything. There was a tanned European couple standing in front of me with long hair, shorts, tie-dye shirts and Birkenstocks.

'I do,' said the girl.

'Who do I have to talk to?'

'That man,' said the girl, pointing to a man sitting at the desk about a foot away from where I was standing, pretending to be engrossed with his paperwork. 'His name's Jorge.'

'Where are you going?'

'Colombia,' the girl said.

'They have a boat?'

'Yes. But he said we have to wait and he will help us.'

'How long ago did he say that?'

'About an hour.'

Jorge, when he finally got round to dealing with me, said he did have a boat, but it wasn't for two days. It was roll-on, roll-off – which is what I wanted since I had heard that if cars go in containers they often get damaged. 'Come back tomorrow lunchtime, meet the customs agent. Price will be eleven hundred dollars. You can pay with traveler's checks.'

I went back down to the car. Tarris was grinning and eating some pineapple. Lenny was smoking.

'Good news,' said Tarris.

'What?'

'We can drive through the Darien Gap. This man here says a Brazilian came through two days ago in a Toyota Corolla.'

'Are there roads?'

'There are tracks. But you can hire guides.'

'You don't need a four-wheel?'

'Not according to Francisco.'

'And what's in it for Francisco?'

'I said you'd give him five bucks.'

'That's right,' said Francisco helpfully. 'He did.'

Later that afternoon Lenny called the American Consulate and spoke to Wesley Pickles. Wesley told him under no circumstance should we attempt to drive through the Gap. The area was controlled by the narco gangsters. It was an independent state. They used it to grow marijuana and coca and policed the area regularly in choppers. We'd be seen and shot on sight. He asked what kind of car we were driving. Lenny told him.

'Forget it,' he said.

We had a meeting. Lenny said, 'If you boys want to drive through there you can do it on your own. I'm not going. I'll meet you down in Bogota or Cartagena. But I'm not *driving* there. You heard what the man said. It's not a smart thing to do.'

We spoke to Anthony. We rang a friend of Tarris's in town. They all said the same thing – don't think about it. We left the hearse up in a big wharf at Cristobal the next day and flew down to Bogota on the Avianca flight. We had a lot to do in Bogota. Tarris was now flat broke. Our entertainment bill through Central America had broken the bank. The only way he could continue was if we generated income.

And here's where old Lenny came up trumps.

'I got this piece of stolen art work,' he said, out of the blue.

'Dear boy,' said Tarris. 'You do?'

'It was given to me.'

'Of course.'

'Bogota is one of *the* major capitals in the world for stolen art. I've been saving this for a special occasion. You sell my painting, Tarris, and I'll lend you ten grand so we can keep moving.'

So we had some business to take care of in Bogota.

37

Bogota is cold. Up on a plateau, 2650 meters higher than the A-C at the Vera Cruz Hotel, Panama City, we felt the chill in the air the minute we walked off the plane. When we collected our bags from the empty carousel, we pulled out more clothes.

'I don't like this, boys,' said Tarris.

'Yeah, man,' said Lenny. 'Let's hope we're not here long. This place is dead.'

The terminal building was empty except for the soldiers. There were more military than passengers. The small crowd from the aircraft filed through customs. All of them were nationals. Colombia did not have a booming tourist trade.

'Taxi, amigo?'

'Como te llamas?'

'Airredo.'

'No, gracias.'

Tarris found some phone booths and started calling hotels to find rooms in the center of town. The taxi-driver looked at me, smiled and held out his hand.

'Propina?' he said. *Propina* is Spanish for tip.

'Why?'

He shrugged.

'No.'

'Cigarrillo?'

I gave him a cigarette and he walked off.

A half-hour later we had cleared customs and immigration and were being driven down a city street into downtown Bogota. We were in the back seat of a little yellow cab with a driver who had racing stripes on his steering-wheel. In Bogota everybody runs the red lights. This means those traversing on the green have to use the horn. Everyone was doing it. In the aftermath of Pablo Escobar's car-bombing campaign, Bogota's traffic cops were more concerned with stationary vehicles than moving ones.

'Buddy,' said Lenny, 'can you *slow* down? You're making me fucking nervous.'

'Qué?'

'Lentamente, asshole! No quiero morir.'

'Sí, sí, sí!' said the driver, ignoring him.

'Mecca!' said Tarris with something akin to wonder as we sped towards the town center. 'I have been looking forward to coming to this country for *years*, boys.'

No prizes for guessing why.

'Looks kinda quiet if you ask me,' said Lenny.

It was ten-thirty at night but the place was dead. It took twenty minutes to get to the center of town from the airport. The hotel was a place called the San Diego in the downtown area of Bogota. It came with bomb-netting on the windows. The hotel was empty – there were keys in all the pigeon-holes. The Colombian dialect of Spanish is a lot more difficult to understand than what we'd been hearing in Central America. Lenny could only understand a few words the concierge was saying. We told him we wanted food and beer. He sent the forty-year-old bell-hop up in the elevator with us to show us our rooms, which were on the seventh and ninth floors. The bins at the end of the hall were filled with broken glass from a recent car bomb. The bell-hop opened each of our doors, went into the room, turned on the wall lights and folded back the bed.

We asked him where we could buy food. He said (and who could blame him?) it was *muy peligroso* to walk on the streets. *Muy peligroso* unless you were a Colombian. If you were

Colombian it was *muy peligroso* but not *so peligroso*. However, he would certainly be glad to try for us. He just happened to know a place that might be –

We paid him. He returned in ten minutes with beer and gin. Twenty minutes later he was back with sandwiches. We settled in Tarris's room and tuned into Colombian television. Colombian television is a lot better than Southern Command television down in Panama. They have great advertisements for a band of super-cops called Los Incorruptibles – the Uncorruptibles. After a thirty-second slot on these boys they had a series of wanted ads for the capture of dangerous narco terrorists. Mug shots of narco gangsters, with a voice-over, a price-tag, and then, supered up, the snappy slogan: Solidaridad Es Seguridad! Solidarity is Security! Power to the People!

We ate. Then we looked at the art work Lenny had Fed-Exed down from New York to Panama. It was a handkerchief. On it was printed a large capitalist symbol.

'*This* is worth twenty thousand dollars?' Tarris asked.

'If we get the right buyer. All you gotta do is find the right buyer, man. Then our money troubles are over.'

'I'll call my man in the morning,' said Tarris.

38

We dressed for the weather: long pants, undershirts, beach shirts, socks, sneakers, long coats. We met down in the dining-room for breakfast. The atmosphere in the place was a lot different from Central America. It was more formal, which seemed strange for a bandit nation. We ordered scrambled eggs, dry toast, coffee and juice.

'Sorta creepy nobody's here, don't you think?' said Lenny.

'Won't be here long, boys,' said Tarris, pieces of paper covering nicks on his chin where he had cut himself shaving. 'All we have to do is find a translator and then we can get rolling.'

The translator wasn't hard to find.

'Shoe-shine?' the kid asked when we walked out of the hotel.

'You speak inglés?' Tarris smiled.

'You can't use *him*,' I said.

'Why not?'

'I doubt he's fourteen. How old are you?'

'Doce!'

'We walk in off the street with this twelve-year-old as our translator, they're going to think –'

'Don't you worry about it, bunje. Leave the business side of things up to me. Besides, he's all that we can afford.'

Tarris looked at the kid and said, 'What are you doing this morning, young man?'

'Qué?'

The gallery was over in the arts district of town. We caught a cab there. We walked in with our little translator, David, sucking his ice-cream.

The dealer – I didn't catch his name, I didn't like him anyway – was around forty, dark-haired, double-breasted Harris tweed suit. He had a plush office with a view of the red roofs of Bogota. Large desk, paintings on the wall, nice European secretary with high heels, long legs, tight skirt, a lot of telephones. He was amused by us. For about three minutes.

With the kid's help Tarris thanked the man for his time,

pulled out the handkerchief and placed it on the desk. Did the man recognize it?

He did.

That's good. Did the man want to buy it?

Maybe.

Maybe? For what kind of price?

Ten grand?

'Done,' said Tarris. 'We'll take it.'

The man said, 'The writing on the bottom here? "To Theo with love." Wasn't Theo the famous gallery owner in New York? You know the one –'

'No,' said Tarris. 'Theo is this man's, ehm, uncle. It was a gift, you see.'

'Un regalo?'

'Sí!'

The man wanted to call the famous gallery owner. Just to make sure . . .

'You know what?' said Tarris, snatching up the hand-kerchief and back-pedalling out of the room. 'Now we know you're interested? We'll be in contact. Maybe do lunch? We have a few more people to see this morning. But we'll be, ehm, in *touch*!'

On the street Tarris said, 'This might take a little longer than I expected.'

That night we found our cabbie connection. He was called Roberto. Roberto showed us all the lively spots in town and hooked us up. The next day he came round to the hotel to ask us to lunch at his house. We were flattered and accepted. Roberto's house was on the outskirts of Bogota. When we got there there was no lunch but there was his beautiful neighbor, a woman introduced as 'muy elegante, muy intelligente, and muy simpática'. She was a doctor of vaccinations and a widow. Tarris fell heavily for this beautiful young lady. Bought her roses. Bought toys for her kid. Took her out for dinner and dancing that night with Lenny and myself and some of her friends. He was very fond of her. They spent that night together. He was very happy. The first free fuck in ages. In the morning she charged him forty bucks.

I flew to Cali to fetch the hearse. I took a bus down to Buenaventura. It hadn't arrived. Gran Flota Colombia, the carrier, expected it in a couple of days. We had arranged to meet at the Hotel Aristi in Cali two days later. But the Hotel Aristi didn't have any rooms when I arrived there, so I went over to the Hotel La Merced. For two days I called the Aristi, but there was no sign of the boys. I walked all over town. I called the embassies and the police authorities. But nobody had seen them, or heard from them. They had disappeared.

39

It was around two on a Saturday afternoon, and I had just about given up hope of seeing the boys again, when I bumped into Lenny. He was walking up the street from the river as I was walking down. He was on his own, wearing his new Latino outfit.

'Where have you been?' I asked him.

'I've been at the Aristi, buddy. Like we *arranged*.'

'That's not what they told me at the front desk. I've been calling that hotel twice a day and they said they had no guest under your name. I thought I'd lost you boys.'

'I've been there, man. All the time.'

But not Tarris. He was still in Bogota trying to sell the painting. We went straight to the Aristi and had a fight with the management. We made such a stink they refunded Lenny the two nights he had stayed just to get us out of the lobby. Lenny booked into my hotel. To celebrate we went down to Avenida Sixta, the main drag in Cali, and slid into the Mexican restaurant there and ordered a large number of frozen margaritas.

About an hour into this margarita run a short, stocky African–Colombian came up to our table. 'You guys from the States?'

'That's right.'

'I *love* Americans,' he said.

'Good for you,' said Lenny.

'My best friend? He from Germany, man.'

'Good for him.'

'When he in Colombia, we like to *par*ty.'

He smiled. He looked friendly enough. Lenny said, 'Is that so?'

'Yeah. We hang out. You like to party?'

'From time to time.'

The man looked over his shoulder. Then he leaned forward and cupped his hand. 'You guys like some coca?'

Well, it was that time in the evening when we were looking for some distractions. And here we were in the cocaine capital of the world . . .

'What's your name?' I asked him.

He thought about this.

'Michael.'

'What do you do for a living, Michael?'

'I'm a tour guide, man.'

'So you work with the tourists?'

'All the time, man. I help 'em out.'

'I'll bet you do. So we can trust you?'

'Trust me? I *love* Americans, man. I party with them all the –'

'What do you think?' I asked Lenny.

'You're not going to dick us, are you, Michael?'

'No.'

'We can trust Michael,' said Lenny.

'How much?' I asked.

'How much you need?'

'A couple of bags to start with.'

'Twenty dollars a bag. You stay right here. Don't you go no place. I fix it up, man.'

So we sat there for an hour and drank a few more margaritas. Then we sat for another hour and drank a lot more margaritas. And coming up to the top of the third hour, when we'd almost forgotten about this African–Colombian, he came back all pleased with himself.

'I got *every*thing ready!' he announced, rubbing his hands together. 'Come with me!'

'What?'

'You guys come with me! We go meet the man.'

'What's wrong with here?' I asked.

'Too much policía, man. Muy peligroso.'

'Muy peligroso' is what everybody says in Colombia if they want to get you to do something you don't want to do.

'What are you suggesting, Michael?' I asked.

'We take a walk.'

'I don't want to take a walk. I'm happy right here.'

'No, man. Too many policía. We must all go.'

'*Both* of us?' I asked.

'Uh-huh.'

'Why both of us?'

'It's better.'

'That doesn't seem all that necessary, does it?' I said. 'I mean, why both of us, Michael? Why not just, you know, *one* of us?'

Michael looked over his shoulder. 'It could take some time. The guy might be late. You know how it is.'

'Where d'you want to go?'

'Little walk.'

'I don't know about this,' I said. 'It doesn't feel good.'

'You got no problem, man,' said Michael. 'We cool.'

And that's when old Lenny chipped in with 'I think we can trust ol' Michael.' And beckoned to the waitress for a couple more margaritas.

'Only one of us is coming with you,' I said.

'There ain't nothing to worry about, man. We amigos. We back here in twenty minutes.'

'Only one of us,' I said.

Michael sighed. 'Okay,' he said.

'But be quick about it, will you?' said Lenny. 'I don't wanna be waiting here all night while you fellas are off having a good time.'

'See you in twenty minutes,' I said.

It was about three hours before I saw Lenny again.

40

'Where have you been?'

I sat down. I had the shakes.

'Michael finked us.'

'Michael *what?*'

'Set us up.'

'Oh, Jesus. How did he do that?'

'It was very easy. We walked up Sixta, went under the underpass, then cut across the square and over the river to the quiet part of town; walking for about twenty minutes, then arriving at a small, empty corner-street bar. We went in. The bar was empty. Just one bar-tender and forty empty tables. We had a beer. I asked for my bags. Michael says relax, we do the switch at the table. So we take the two cold Pokers to the table, I give him the money, he gives me the bags, I get up to leave and he says, "Amigo? Finish your beer."'

And Lenny said, 'You didn't suspect nothin'?'

'I was curious if what I thought might happen was going to happen. So I thought I'd go to the bathroom, hide the bags, come back, finish my beer and see how things turned out. And I was just about to do that, too, when —'

'Cops?'

'Seven in uniform, one, a café-au-lait guy, in plain clothes. They come running through the doors, yelling and pointing their guns. Michael bursts into fits of tears saying he doesn't want to go to jail, he can't believe this bad luck, how will his poor mama survive — he doesn't want me to think he set me up. So, they come flying over, shout at me to stand up, put the hands in the air and I start thinking, well, there you go. Piss-poor judgement. When are you going to learn?

'They empty my pockets. Out pop the little bags. The

mulatto smiles. He says to me, "For this amount of coca, gringo, you can go to jail eight to fifteen years in Colombia –"'

'Oh shit,' said Lenny.

'So I tell the man there must be a little misunderstanding here. He opens the bag, dips his little pinkie in it and says, "It's no sugar, eh, amigo?" I tell him I want to call the consul. He says I can't call the consul. He says right now I can't even blow my nose unless he says I can. He lets me sweat while his boys rifle through my wallet, count out the cash and give it to him with my passport and my credit card. "Fifteen years, amigo," he says. "That's a long, long time in a jail."

'We go outside the bar, just the two of us, he sits me on a wall and then he comes out with that great Colombian line, "we are all muy intelligente, la vida es muy dura but en la vida there is always a solution . . ."'

'How much?' Lenny asked.

'One thousand dollars. I tell him a thousand is a very fair price to stay out of jail fifteen years. As we're sitting there some guy in a green uniform and an orange bib comes over with the handcuffs. The mulatto says that won't be necessary, he's going to cooperate. He asked me where the money was. I said it was back in my hotel room. He says we'll go to your hotel and I think, as long as we're not going to the police station we're doing terrific. He bundles me and our friend Michael in the back of an unmarked car. With four motor-cycle outriders we shoot crosstown. Problem is, I only have twenty-five dollars in the room. I don't have the thousand I said I had. But I need time to think. These boys are on edge and it takes me a little while to work out that they're scared of Los Incorruptibles. Every minute they're with me, they're putting their necks on the line. Cali is a small town. Not many gringos. We get to the hotel. But they don't stop *outside*. They stop around the corner. The mulatto says to me, "You get the money but don't try anything stupid." I don't have my passport nor my wallet – he's confiscated them. I run into the hotel, go up to the room, grab my traveler's checks, write you a note which I leave with the concierge, then run back out to the street, thinking I'll tell him we can go to a change shop and change some checks, he'll be fine with that idea. So I get back to the car, he bundles me in the back seat, says, "Where's my money?" and I tell him, there's been a little problem with the money, because you must have taken it. I show him the checks. He hits the roof. It's seven-fifteen. All the change shops shut at seven. Luckily, he's a greedy little bastard and he still wants his money. He's put himself to a lot of trouble and risk setting this all up – the empty bar, finding you, me, paying that snitch Michael. So instead of taking me down to the station, he says we're going to do the hotels. I say you can't change money at the hotels unless you're a guest. He says, "Right! You will *be* a guest, amigo."

'Hotels will only change a hundred dollars for guests, so a quick calculation, ten rooms – that's a thousand dollars in hotel bills for a thousand in cash.'

'This hurts.'

'The first hotel we go to is the Inter-Continental. The Inter-Continental hotel is the most expensive hotel in Cali. We park across the street. I get out. Then I realize I can't get a room without a credit card and a passport. I tell him this. He thinks about it. He doesn't have a choice. He gives me them, I go in the lobby, I walk up to the desk, I take a room, I change fifty, and now I'm starting to think about how to get away. I leave my passport with the concierge; next hotel I'm going to skip out the back, loop back to the Inter-

Continental, pick up the passport and run. As soon as I walk back out the front, the car screeches up outside, the mulatto jumps out, shoves me in the back, the car shoots away from the curb and he starts shouting for money. I show him what I've got. He snatches it, counts it and stuffs it in his pocket. The driver – he's in on this – asks how much they got. When he's told it's only fifty, both of them start swearing and shouting. Luckily, the next hotel they want to go to is the Aristi –'

' – the one where we had the shouting match with the management.'

'The very same. We pull up nearby, then I tell him I can't go in that hotel. I explain.'

'And he says?'

'He doesn't. He looks at his watch. We've been running around together for about forty-five minutes. Forty-five minutes is a long long time. He says we'll meet in the square opposite the Aristi, ten tomorrow, and I can give him what I owe him. Then he confiscates my traveler's checks.'

'All of them?'

'Yeah, but this is the good part. He doesn't ask me to countersign and I don't say a word. So I'm just about to get out the car when I realize it's a twenty-five-minute walk to the hotel, a forty-minute walk here, and I don't have a peso in my pocket because he's got them all in his. I ask him if he'd consider lending me my cab fare. He won't. He drops me back at the hotel. As I'm getting out the car he warns me not to keep him waiting in the morning and tells me he's going to have me watched.'

'We have to get out of town. Immediately . . .'

*

Seven hours later, around four-thirty in the morning, we were walking across the buffed marble lobby of the Inter-Continental Hotel: me, Lenny and two nice young ladies we'd met palm-reading at the Baly-Hi night-club, heading past the *fica* trees and the bamboo furniture for the night-desk, hoping to get up to the room and the mini-bar I'd paid for earlier. We were going to leave town but then Lenny said, 'Be mad with me, man. Enough is enough. I'm going back to New York.'

'You're *what*?'

'I'm going home, man. I'm getting out of this nuthouse. If you were smart, *you'd* do the same!'

'I'm going to Rio,' I said. 'You should come with me.'

To my eyes, we weren't really in a *lot* of trouble until ten the following morning. Since this was now Lenny's *last* night, we had to go out. To throw any greedy narco cops off the scent, we craftily moved hotels a couple of times. Eventually we moved down on to Sixta and into a cheap little place right opposite the Mexican joint where Michael had set us up. We took rooms in the back, then slipped down on to the street and had a large number of cocktails at the bar next door. Then we went to the Baly-Hi for the evening. Now we were back at Cali's exclusive Inter-Continental hotel, four-thirty in the morning, peso-less, with some important calls to take care of and two nice young ladies for company.

The management at Cali's Inter-Continental are not the world's friendliest. It probably doesn't help much when their guests are wearing micro-minis, tube tops with tassles in all the right places and high-heeled shoes with little bows on their toes. María, my date, had her right leg in a cast all the way up to the top of her thigh, the result of a dancing ac-cident. Every step the young beauty took across the enormous marble lobby, the little steel cap on her one black high heel rang out: Clack! Clack! Clack! which gave the night-manager plenty of time to get his best shitty look ready for us.

'Sí?' he said.

I told him I had a room here.

He didn't think it possible – not in the outfits we were wearing: Lenny in his pointy Beatle boots, brown shiny pants, white Guayabera shirt with about a million creases in it and a pair of one-armed mock tortoise Ray-Bans in his hair. I had my beach hat, my Stan Smiths, a check shirt, faded blue pants and my Mace box.

'Have a look,' I said. 'Room uno uno tres.'

'No! No puedes haber las chicas en tu habitación!'

We couldn't have the girls in the room.

'Why not?'

'Seguridad,' he said.

At this point Lenny started to get a little agitated. He leaned heavily over the marble counter, narrowed his blood-shot eyes and snapped, '*You're* worried about security? What do you think *I'm* worried about? I'm not even a Colombian! These are my *bodyguards*, for Chrissakes!'

'That's right,' I said, slipping into the familiar role of fellow-combatant. Around this time of day, four-thirty in the a.m., the foe always ended up being snotty hotel people complaining about the guest problem. 'These girls are *protecting* us!'

'No puedes,' the man said. It went back and forth like this until the manager appeared.

'What is the problem here?' he asked.

'This man,' I said. 'He says we can't have our friends up to my room.'

The manager looked at the four of us. 'Yes, I can see why.'

For the next ten minutes we kicked up quite a stink, but he'd heard it all before and from much richer, more sober and more articulate clients than us. He wouldn't move an inch. But he did say, 'If you don't want to stay, we will refund your money!' And I thought: you will? That's kind. But Lenny wasn't interested in refunds.

'*I . . . wanna . . . stay . . . here!*' he said, banging his big fist on the counter.

'You can,' said the manager. 'But not your guests.'

No mini-bar, no power-shower, no bubble-bath at five in the morning. A tough break. I asked the night-manager to give me back my passport which I had given to them earlier. No room fee. A good night's work. Only we had nowhere to sleep. But then Lenny said, 'Hey, don't we already *have* rooms?'

41

I was awake and rolling over and my watch said it was nine forty-eight, and the overhead fan was just stirring up enough of a wind to stop the sweat dribbling down my forehead. As I rolled over and began to savour one or two of the night's high points, the warning bells went off and I remembered: it's nine *forty-eight*. That would make it twelve minutes before Cali's young investigator would be thinking: the little bastard has stood me up.

Running down the hall, trying to pull my pants on, I banged on Lenny's door. '*Lenny?*' I shouted. '*Lenny! Get up!* Let's go! C'mon! C'mon! C'mon! It's ten-to-ten!'

Five minutes later, bags still in the room because we didn't have the time to pack them, we were down on Sixta looking at a bunch of soldiers standing nearby and I started to think: do I know you, gentlemen? Did we meet yesterday in an empty little corner bar over the other side of the river?

Lenny said, 'What the hell are we doing?'

'Getting out of town.'

'We should have done that twelve hours ago.'

'I know.'

'It's *Sunday*. All the change shops in Cali are *shut* on Sunday. Where are we going to *get* money?'

I tried to think. Not easy. Eight years in a stinking Colombian jail. Hangover. Tylenol bottle tipped down the toilet when reaching for it. Not easy.

An idea arrived.

'The airport,' I said.

'What if they're *watching* the airport?'

'They won't. Not for that sort of money.'

'Hey, they *kill* down here for twenty bucks! You think he's not going to have one of his pals watch the airport? Anyway, I can't change more money.'

'Why not?' I asked.

'I don't *have* more money. The only way we can get money is if *you* change some of *your* traveler's checks.'

But there was another more immediate and pressing problem: no cabs. When we finally flagged one down and sank into the small back seat feeling a general easing of the bowels, we soon discovered the change shops at the airport were also shut on Sunday. And now we didn't even have enough money to pay the cab. Only one thing left to do . . .

'Señor?'

'Qué?'

'The Aristi, por favor.'

Lenny said, 'Wait a minute. We're not *allowed* in the Aristi, remember? We got kicked *out* of the Aristi, two days ago. We can't go to the Aristi.'

'We have no choice.'

'This is fucked up,' said Lenny. 'This is really, really fucked up.'

We headed back to town. The only trouble with this plan was that the Hotel Aristi happened to be right opposite the spot where I had my appointment with Cali's young investigator whom I was now twenty minutes late meeting. I slid on to the floor.

'What are you doing?' Lenny asked.

'Hiding. You change the money. I'll wait here.'

Lenny looked down at me witheringly and said, 'I told you we should have left last night.'

'Go get the money,' I said.

Lenny got out of the cab. Squatting on the floor, squeezed down tight behind the tiny bench-seat, I waited. Lenny was back a few minutes later.

'They wouldn't do it.'

'Why *not*?'

'Because we're not taking *rooms* there.'

'Why don't you take rooms?'

'I tried. They won't let me.'

'Did you tell 'em we're desperate? A matter of –'

'It's over. We should have gotten out of here last night. This is *your* fault.'

'*My* fault?'

'*I* said we should leave town last night. And now –'

'Señor?' I said. 'Avenida Sixta, por favor.'

'Are you listening to me?' Lenny asked.

'Always.'

'So what are we going to do?'

'I'm thinking about it.'

Back on Avenida Sixta, I paid the cab with my last ten-dollar bill. In the hotel, they were having a power-cut and the room temperature was up in the high nineties.

'All we need,' I said, 'is a hotel that we can pay for with a credit card. With room service so we can eat, a mini-bar so we can drink, and access to a telephone so we can book a plane *out* of here –'

'You got any ideas?'

An hour later Lenny called me on the telephone.

'I'm here,' he said.

'Did you see him?' I asked.

'No.'

'How about police? Lot of *police* around the place?'

'There's *always* a lotta cops.'

'How is it over there?'

'Listen to this. I'm lying on a double-bed, the A-C is up at ten, I gotta vodka-tonic in my hand, the mini-bar is stacked, room service is bringing up some huevos and bacon, I've just had a hot shower and I'm watching *Edward Scissorhands* on cable.'

'With or without sub-titles?'

'Who fucking cares?'

Lenny was back at the Inter-Continental.

'What are you doing?' he asked.

The power was back on but the fan had quit. The bathroom had flooded. There was no Coca-Cola machine in the lobby. There was no room-service, no mini-bar, no A-C, and any minute now I expected to hear the pitter-patter of tiny jackboots running along the hall.

'I'll be right over,' I said.

'Hey,' said Lenny, helpfully, 'if I don't see you in one hour, man, I'll call the consul for you.' Then he laughed.

42

Cali is not an easy place to leave. Two days later, five in the morning or thereabouts, we were still there, still up, but this was good. The way it had to be, in fact. At some point everything was going to fall *apart*. Or Lenny would finally catch a plane. Either way it would be finished.

For the third day in a row, Lenny was booked on a flight to Bogota with a connection back to New York City and it looked like there weren't any obstacles to stop him. He'd said that two days earlier, of course. But now he was actually packing, not thinking about where to go next. I was watching him throw a few things into that canvas holdall of his, the one with the bust zip.

'Well,' he said closing the bag. 'This is it, I guess.'

'You sure you don't want to come to carnaval? Be happy to take you.'

'I'm going home. It's the right time for me to go home. I feel ready for a good rest from you.'

'You should come. It's gonna be a lot of fun.'

Lenny grabbed his bag. I put him in the cab. After all this time together it was not a sentimental farewell. He gave me the finger.

'Call me, asshole,' he said. 'Let me know how you are. And do me a favor?'

'What?'

'Get out of here.'

I closed the cab door. The driver started the car and pulled away. I watched Lenny's big face shrink in the back of the cab window. I watched until it was gone and there was nothing left to see. Then I went up to the room. There was a power-cut again and it was dark. On my pillow was a crumpled piece of paper. It was a little sketch. The picture was of the three of us, sitting in the front seat of the hearse. The driver's shape was drawn in a single unbroken line. The two pas-sengers sitting alongside were drawn in dotted silhouettes – as if they were ghosts.

Good luck, it said. *Love, Lenny.*

43

There is nothing quite like the threat of a long period of incarceration in a stinking foreign jail to help focus the mind on the – until this point – relatively relaxed attitude toward travel arrangements. As soon as Lenny was heading off to the airport, I slipped down Sixta avoiding all eye contact with the military and police and waited for the banks to open. Then I caught the first cab out of town.

Riding out of town, I made a little vow to myself. This sort of behavior would have to stop. It was time to be sensible and responsible. The only road up from Buenaventura, the port where the hearse was now held, to the Ecuadorian fron-tier, came through the center of Cali. The important thing to remember when coming back through Cali was not to stop at the Baly-Hi to see the girls. Just keep going, preferably at night when the town's crooked police force were tucked up in bed dreaming of stupid tourists . . .

44

The customs services in Buenaventura pride themselves on a new philosophy of modernization and honesty: I noticed a typed letter addressed to all employees posted on the notice-board as we walked in. The customs office is an enormous old Spanish colonial governmental building. Built around a large courtyard, it has balconies on every floor, and hundreds of offices. Josefina, a big, cheerful woman, was my customs agent. I found her in the book. We went up to the second floor, banged on a number of different office doors, got different stamps for different pieces of paper required to get a car imported into the country, and then visited the office of the chief of customs for the port of Buenaventura. We had to talk to him about the law of either having to travel with a police escort to the Ecuadorian border or having a *libreta de pase de aduana*. I didn't have a *libreta* – a form of bond. And I didn't want to travel with a policeman. They were too costly one way or another.

The chief of customs had a vast office for one man. It had wooden floors, tall ceilings, a number of large interconnected rooms, a secretary, and an old air-conditioning unit wheezing away in a window. He was a well-dressed man. He sat behind a big desk in front of a shipping map of the world, talking on the telephone. Three young officials in neatly pressed short-sleeved shirts and pants waited nervously for instructions.

For twenty minutes the chief talked on the phone. He looked at the wall, he looked at the map, he played with his pencil, but he never acknowledged we were sitting opposite him. When he finished, he asked one of his juniors what we were doing in his office. My case was explained in brief. I told them I was a college professor – academics are respected in

Latin America – in transit to Brazil, but couldn't get my car out from the port because I didn't want to pay the $5000 in duty without the *libreta*, nor the $400 to have a soldier sit next to me for two days, demanding money, cigarettes, cassettes and dinners.

'It is very difficult,' said the chief.

The three juniors nodded. Very difficult indeed.

'In Colombia, we have import taxes. Without a bond or police escort you could sell the car and then leave. That is why there is a bond.'

The juniors smiled in unison. I could tell what they were thinking; the chief is one smart cookie – that's why he's the chief. I pulled out my passport and asked him to look at the stamps.

'In Central America,' I said, 'they have this system to guarantee that a traveller won't sell his car. They gave you this stamp in your passport, you see.' I showed him. 'It shows that you arrived in the country with a particular type of vehicle and therefore you must leave with one.'

He studied it.

'This is modern.' He showed it to the office juniors. They commended his opinion. 'We do not have a stamp like this.'

'I know. But maybe you could make one? Write out my details in ink like the Hondurans have done? Then your colleagues at Ipiales will know that I can only leave the country if I'm driving my Cadillac.'

'Carroza,' he smiled.

'Carroza,' I replied.

The chief flicked through the pages, then smoothed his patterned tie against his silk shirt.

'Mexico, Guatemala, El Salvador, Honduras, Nicaragua, Costa Rica – they all have this stamp?'

'They do.'

He summoned the most senior junior, a tidy little man, late twenties in a short-sleeved dress-shirt. They spoke. It was agreed. He made a copy of the stamp, filled in the details, signed some more of Josefina's papers, and said, 'I can only give you two days to leave Colombia.'

'One is all I need,' I told him.

45

When I saw my hearse again I felt elated. I was naked without my black beast and I had missed her. Not having those two drunks around any more would allow a more focused attempt at getting down to Brazil. It would be good to drive alone and I was looking forward to it.

The hearse was parked at the end of a long line of imported combis and Japanese pick-ups lined up on the dock. I pointed the car out to Josefina and grinned.

'Mi carroza!' I said proudly.

'Loco gringo,' she said.

But the car had been damaged in transit – the wheelskirts were dented and the front end had been banged. And they'd stolen anything of any value. Josefina said there was nothing we could do about the damage. I could shout at Gran Flota Colombia, the carrier, but there was little chance of compensation without legal action and even if there was legal action they'd drag it out for months. I had eighteen days to get down to Brazil.

It took four-and-a-half hours to get the car out of the port. After stamps from various offices had been collected, a payment in cash made at an office window for port tax, the key fetched from a safe in a hut by the main gates, the car had to be jumped since somebody had left the lights on. I enlisted the help of a couple of soldiers. We plugged some leads on a Land-Cruiser, but not my leads because someone had stolen those. They moved a couple of combis out of the way, to allow me to reverse down the long line of automobiles, past the mountains of containers, the giant railway cranes, the fork-lifts rushing about the docks in the floodlights, to join the lines of tractor-trailers and old trucks waiting to clear their freight through the port gates. Nine-thirty that night I cleared the gates of the port of Buenaventura.

I pulled the car out on to the dark street. I slid a tape in the deck, turned it up, wound the window right down, lit a cigarette, and pointed the nose of the car on the only road leading out of town.

I stole into Cali sometime around two in the morning. Around four, somewhere way out in the dark countryside up high in the Cordillera, I pulled on to a dirt shoulder behind some old trucks to sleep. It was the best sleep I'd had in days.

46

The *libreta de pase de aduana* was going to cause a lot of problems unless I could come up with a decent cover story. I had tried to buy one from the Venezuelan Automobile Club when we were back in Panama, but when I called them up, I was told the man in charge of the sale, Mr Juan Petri, had died. Nobody else in the office was doing them any more. Ecuador and Bolivia, like Colombia, required the *libreta* in order to drive through the country. No *libreta*, no *entrar*.

At customs at Tulcan on the Ecuadorian side of the border

with Colombia late the next day, I told the gentleman in the olive uniform sitting in his chair gazing vacantly out at the people milling to and fro in the market by the frontier that I had recently had a most terrible piece of luck. I was robbed. In Panama. Thieves broke into my car, stole my wallet, my traveler's checks, my credit cards and my *libreta* which I bought for 2000 bucks in New York City . . .

The soldier was not surprised. He told me Panama was full of thieves. I said that I was on my way to Rio and that the chief of the port at Buenaventura had been very accommodating. He'd made up this little stamp for me to allow me to get through the country, you see? I showed it to him. He agreed to do the same. It all worked beautifully until I drove past his hut a half-hour later. Then he came rushing out and demanded to know what charity I was raising money for driving a *hearse*.

I hadn't thought about this. I offered him a cigarette. He loved his Marlboros. I lit his, lit one for myself and then asked him if he'd like the pack. He smiled. I gave him the pack. Then I had an idea. I told him the charity was trying to raise money to protect a small cemetery in Manhattan. Developers wanted to erect a building on this cemetery.

A sacrilege, he said.

I agreed. I said this cemetery also happened to be of great personal significance because my grandfather, God rest his soul, was buried there. That's why I was driving this hearse. To raise money to protect the family plot.

He let me go. I had now crossed nine borders. I had three to go.

After visiting eight countries I had begun to notice that in every major city in Latin America there is always one part of town that has all the car parts stores – the *auto repuestos* district. In Quito, the Ecuadorian capital, it was in the downtown district. I limped into Quito without brakes six hours after crossing the border. But the garage I selected – it didn't have a name – didn't carry my type of brake pads. Nobody in Quito carried pads to fit the calipers on a '73 Cadillac hearse. But this wasn't a problem.

In South America everyone can fix cars. You can break down in the middle of nowhere and if you're riding in something interesting you'll have five people under the hood helping you fix it in no time. They know cars and they know how to fix them even when they don't have the right parts. The hearse was put up on a lifter and raised slowly. The chief of the garage marveled at how heavy it was. He said he hoped my car did not break his old lifter. The lifter spat and huffed and teetered. When it was high enough, the mechanics took off the front wheels and disks, pulled out the brake calipers and then walked down the street to the brake shop where they custom-cut pads to fit. It took an afternoon and about five dollars. I had three spare sets made. The next day I left for the beach.

One of the many assets of driving around in an old funeral car is that people are always curious. I had a flat the next morning down on the Pacific coast and as I was laid out under the car in the dirt trying to jack it up, a surfer called François cycled up and started talking to me. François was somewhere around thirty, tanned, with long matted bleached blond hair, no shirt, no shoes, just shorts and a little colorful macramé wristlet and a small back-pack. His face was lean and friendly. He said he and some of his friends had come to Las Montañitas to spend the winter surfing (Las Montañitas was where I had broken down). François spoke English with a Hawaiian accent. He wanted to know what I was doing here, how I got here, where I was going, all of that. We talked. He insisted I come down the beach and have a beer with him and his friends.

I had not spoken English to anybody since putting Lenny in a cab back in Cali. The idea of sitting in the shade with a cold beer talking English instead of babbling pidgin Spanish with corrupt policemen was very pleasant. I threw the flat in the back, then followed François down the dirt track to the beach. I parked in front of some *cabanas* behind a beach bar.

The surfers – Alex, Jean and a few others – were playing Scrabble when we walked in. Surfers love Scrabble. Alex the Australian had a saying he used frequently that day when looking out from his table in the shade to the bright sun on the dark blue sea and the foaming white water breaking on the reef off-shore. 'Cor-du-roy, mate,' he said. 'That's what we want. Lined up like fucking cor-du-roy.' Translation: when the swell marches down on the reef a couple of hundred yards off-shore, it makes clean separate lines, one after the other, right across the bay. These lines, regularly spaced, look like corduroy.

These surfers had a restful existence. They rose early with the sun, went into the water for two or three hours, and came out when the wind picked up around ten. The wind disturbed the faces of the waves. So they waited, and played Scrabble and read and wrote postcards, until the wind dropped off as it did most days around four in the tropics. When the wind drops, the sea glasses over except for the corduroy out in the bay. Under these conditions the wave breaks cleanly on the reef. The surfers would then return to the sea and stay there until sunset, riding the waves.

François loved the *carroza*. He told me I was doing something he'd always wanted to do himself. I said he was doing something I had wanted to try, too.

He said, 'If you like the serf, we serf later! I teach you!'

So, late that afternoon, I went surfing for the first time in my life. With reflection I'd say it's probably not such a good idea after a few beers. But anyway, I stood by the hearse late in the afternoon as the boys arrived with their boards under their arms – François, Alex, Jean. O'Neal and Quicksilver board shorts; little colorful macramé on brown wrists. All fit-looking. No fat, muscles, long blond dread curls and that wide-eyed, wonder-filled expression common to zealots, Jehovah's Witnesses and surfers expecting a good afternoon in the water. Right then I started to think that these boys looked fit enough to swim to California and wondered how fit you have to be to do this sport.

François was holding a board for me.

'You serf on this,' he said.

'What is it?'

'My long board.'

I took hold of the long board. It was light for its size, about eight-and-a-half feet in length. On one side it had a beautiful flamed paint job, orange, yellow and red, and a lumpy surface of clear wax. On the other it had three fins set in a triangle at the tail. On the bottom it had a number of channels cut into it. The nose was blunt, the lines much fuller than the smaller boards they held under their arms, and it was thicker – the rail was about two inches, not the inch of their own. Attached to the tail end was a long urethane leash and a velcro cuff.

''E,' François said, pointing at the cuff, 'go on the leg.'

I put him on the leg. Alex and Jean started trotting toward the sea. (I don't know why, but all surfers run to the sea. It's a fact. Maybe it's a habit from running over hot sand.) On the water there were already two surfers paddling out. We walked down to the water's edge. It was, François told me, looking out to sea, with his left hand shading his eyes from the glare, perfect: four- to six-foot, light off-shore breeze. Beautiful conditions.

Jean and Alex launched into the water, paddling into the sun that was low and red and swollen. I had my first surfing lesson. François instructed me to put my board on a shallow bank of sand with the nose pointing down the hill. I put the board on the sand, then stood back.

'You lie!' he instructed.

I lay on the surfboard.

'You get up!'

I got one leg up and was getting up on the other, when he said, 'No, no, no! One smooth moov'ment! Watch!'

François took my place.

'You put the hands like this,' he said, moving his hands on the rail to a position in line with his shoulders. 'Then – oopla!'

And he was standing upright in the surfer's crouch; one fluid and athletic movement.

'You see?'

I nodded.

'Good! You try!'

I lay down on my belly.

'Show me the paddle!' François asked.

I showed him the paddle.

'Now the wave arrive, what you do?'

I pushed up with my hands. I whipped my legs underneath me. I assumed the position. In the crouch, left arm pointing down the face of the wave, right arm cocked.

'There!' I said.

'Is good,' said François, 'if you want the wipe-out. And we pick your teeth with coral. Your feet must be like this! Not so close! The right foot 'ere! To make the steering. Try again!'

I tried again.

And again.

And again.

'There!' I said, crouched in the surfer's tuck, one fluid movement to the feet, right foot squarely on the tail, right leg bent, right arm ready to punch the wave's lights out. 'Good?'

François shrugged.

'Let's go,' he said.

Nothing to it, I thought. Going to be easier than eating tortillas.

'Next fing to know,' said François as we walked down to the beach, 'is to make the paddle. When you are on the board you must have the front comme ça!'

He angled the fingers on his palm pointing upwards. 'If he make underwater? Boff! You wipe out, bro.'

'Keep the nose above the water?'

'Exactement! And when you come to the big serf –' he indicated a wave a couple of feet above my head – 'you fink too big? Abandon the board. Okay? You swim to the floor, you wait for the wave to pass, et puis, you retourn.'

'How do you know when you can come up?'

'When you have no breath!' said François, laughing.

He picked up the board. 'Now,' he said, holding the board in front of him and looking over his shoulder as if he was about to catch a wave, 'to catch the wave. One must make the position. Not straight down but to one side. The wave, he arrive *'ere.'* He indicated some spot about two feet behind the board. 'He is breaking. You paddle, paddle, paddle. The board, now he go the same speed –' a complicated set of hand gestures explained the relation and aspect of the board to the advancing wave '– the wave catch you. Et puis, oopla! You go! You jump to the feet like we make? Voilà! Sairfeeng, bro!'

François slapped my back.

'Comprends?' he asked.

'Easy,' I said.

François laughed.

We sat on the hot sand and attached the urethane leashes to our ankles. Out on the reef I saw Jean start paddling as this swollen lump of water rose up behind him. I saw the wave gather the board and rider up. I watched him slip to his feet (in the one fluid movement). I watched him charge down the face of this big wave, make a deep turn in the pit at the bottom, lay up a great wall of spray and lean the body heavily into the white water breaking in front and a little behind him. There must have been a six- or seven-foot face on this wave. He pulled back up into its face, put his hand into the wall to slow his speed, and then disappeared behind a waterfall of tumbling white water.

François let out a shrill whistle of approval. He shook his hand above his head as if he had touched a hot coal.

'*Mental barrel!*' shouted François. 'Mental barrel!'

I thought: be doing that in a minute. Mental barrel.

'Ready?' François asked me.

'Can't wait,' I said.

'Bon! Let's go!'

I watched François take a couple of steps into the shallows and then dive, bringing the board out from under his arm to put under his chest before it struck the water. Easy, I thought, taking a running dive at the water, getting the board out from under my arm to pull under my chest and landing on it. Then I fell off.

'Doucement, bro,' said François, grinning, when I surfaced.

I tried *doucement*. I put the board on the water, pointed the nose out at the incoming chop and crawled aboard like an old lady. This was a lot easier. But surfboards aren't comfortable nor particularly stable.

'Allons!' François called. He was sitting astride his board, the nose pointing up at the sky, and waving.

We set off, stroking through the warm water to the channel that would take us out and round the back of the reef. As we paddled closer, the ripples in the channel became little waves and the little waves soon became bigger waves. When the first sizeable stream of white water came bubbling down our path, I heard François shout, 'Dooc-dive, bro!' and watched him sit up, put his weight over the rails of the board and make the nose submerge. Then I don't know what he did: put a knee or something on the tail and submerged that too. It took maybe two seconds. The white water rolled over the top of him.

Later, when I was busy draining water from different parts of my head, François explained that what I had observed was something called a duck-dive. The principle is simple. Underneath every wave is a moving channel of water. If you can get yourself and the board into this stream it's like taking the subway. You and the board get in the stream, are channeled under the wave, and pop out on the other side in clean water. If you can do this properly you can go fifteen, twenty feet in this stream without lifting a finger. If you can't, you get swept back, which is what happened to me. Swept back, turned over and separated from the board.

I surfaced. François was a long way ahead of me now, sitting astride his board, bobbing up and down on the water with the easy confidence of a duck. Another wave broke. I was pushed further inshore. I clambered aboard, pointed in the right direction, paddled, another wave broke and I was pushed back to where I started. This went on for about ten minutes before there was a flat patch. Then I paddled like stink. François thought this was very funny.

'A little harder than I anticipated,' I said.

'Is a good sport?'

'If you're a fish.'

A half-hour later we were finally out around what they call the back of the break. My arms were tight, my shoulders felt like they were filled with sand.

'Now z' wicked fun start!'

Drowning stinks. Once the panic has passed it's quite nice, like they say. Peaceful. You can open your eyes and enjoy it, but before you get to that stage you have a big panic.

I'd fallen off three waves successfully without getting close to nailing the take-off when I was caught inside. Caught inside means you are about to have a near-death experience. I was sitting on the board, watching everyone else stroke off for the horizon, wondering why they were all sprinting like maniacs, when I heard someone shout, 'Out the back!' And then I saw them: these big moving mountains. When a big set rolls in, the waves break further out than usual – in this instance about twenty feet further out from the place the rest of the sets had broken in the fifteen minutes I had been bobbing up and down tipping off a surfboard. So, with my arms windmilling through the water like jet turbines, I bolted for the horizon and had just made it over the shoulders of the first two smaller waves in the set, was climbing up the face of the third wave – it seemed to me to be about as tall as a house – felt it get steeper, saw the lip crumble above me, pass over me, and for a brief moment I thought I'd made it, I was safe, the wave had gone through, but then I had this freefall sensation. Backwards. This is what the boys call going over the falls. Going over the falls is like base-jumping back-wards. I went over, got sucked under, thrown up, tumbled around; I tried to keep my head up and my body relaxed because of the shallow water on the reef, and then I'm not sure what happened. Flipped this way, that way, one leg here, the other there, with this board that was trying to rip my leg off. And no air. I didn't know which way was up or down. I struck for the surface. Wrong way . . .

I don't suppose I was under the water more than fifteen seconds but that was long enough. I surfaced just in time to watch another wave about to break, a great convex wall of green and white water collapsing on my head. I dove for the bottom, flipped over on to my back, cocked the leg with the leash attached and waited. Being deeper down on the reef made a small but noticeable difference. The underwater turbulence was not as bone-wrenching as being caught upstairs, but almost. It was three more of these dives to the bottom before the set passed through and there was enough of a lull to allow me to grab hold of the board and rest.

François came paddling over. 'Next time I say, "Out the back!" you must paddle a little quicker, uh?'

I stayed out another twenty minutes but after all the paddling and drowning I'd been doing I had lost all my enthusiasm for the sport, and when I finally caught a wave and felt the great thrill of rushing down its face – it's sort of like falling off a house – I hadn't the strength to push up off the board and leap to my feet in the one fluid movement required. I pitched head over the front of the board, banged my shoulder on the reef and retired to the bar for a cigarette and a drink.

49

The fat Peruvian in the tight white T-shirt, the combat pants and the polished boots didn't think much of my theory that he should let me into his country without a *libreta de pase de aduana* just because it said he should in my guide-book. He said because I didn't have the documents, I was going to have to drive to the main crossing at Tombes. I didn't want to drive to Tombes. Tombes was twelve hours back across mountains, the way I had come from Los Montanittas. And during that night roaming through empty Ecuadorian mountain country, the back wheel had fallen off, shearing four wheel studs, while I was chasing a bus to keep awake. Now all four wheels were secured by only four studs, not the regulation five (a stud had to be taken from each of the three remaining wheels to secure the fourth wheel back to the hub). Also, the transmission wouldn't shift out of L2, the suspension was banging and there was an intermittent whining sound from the engine which I suspected to be a piston ring failure, so I wanted the car down in Lima for a service as fast as possible, to be sure of making carnaval.

But the Peruvian said I had to go back to Tombes.

I walked back across the bridge to talk to the Ecuadorian officials. The chief and his friends commiserated with me, told me it was what you must expect with Peruvians. He suggested I go see their consul in town and instructed a young Chiclet salesman to show me the consul's office. We drove up the dirt road to town.

They were shutting for the day when I arrived. The male secretary showed me to a waiting-room. Five minutes later I was led into the consul's office. I explained I was having a little problem with customs officials at the border.

The consul asked me which one.

I described him.

'I know him,' said the consul. 'A peasant!'

I told the consul I'd been driving through the night, I was tired but I needed to get across the border today, if possible, because I was in a very big hurry.

'It is not good to be in a hurry.'

'I know.'

'But I shall give you a letter. He will have to let you pass with my authorization!'

'Thank you.'

I headed back down the muddy road to the border with the letter. I parked on the Ecuadorian side of the bridge, went and waved to all the friendly Ecuadorian officials, crossed the bridge, ignored the Indian money-changers, and went back to see the soldier, another Indian. I showed him the piece of paper from the consul instructing him to let me enter the country with my car. He shook his head. He threw the piece of paper on his desk. The gist was: big deal. I'm boss around here. Not that dink up in town. Beat it.

'Señor,' I said. 'Puedo hablar con tu en privado?'

'Claro.'

He took me into his office and closed the door. I gave him the line the Colombians used on me – we are all *muy intelligente*. But *en la vida* always there is *un solucion*, etc. I told him it would be my great pleasure to make the man a little *regalo* – present.

He smiled.

It cost me seventy bucks to get him to fudge the paperwork to get into Peru.

50

The dog wasn't doing much. It walked out into the road 300 yards ahead of me, on the outskirts of town, stopped, then sat on its haunches to scratch fleas. A truck came down the street. The truck-driver didn't slow for the dog. He didn't move the big truck to one side, either. He ran straight over the animal, the front axle striking the dog's skull, the dog's body turning over, being dragged a little while, then bouncing up and hitting the drive-shaft and the rear axle. The truck accelerated. The driver was looking in his door-mirror and laughing. Two hundred meters back, I had just passed a sign: *Bienvenidos a Peru!*

I drove through the night. There were many police and army checkpoints on the road. They all had their line. 'In

Peru, tinted windows are against the law, amigo.' Or, 'To drive alone in Peru is very dangerous, you need protection.' Some were much more honest. 'Give me money if you want to continue, señor.'

All through that moonless night I watched the little stone mile-markers on the Pan-American highway diminish and hoped the transmission wouldn't seize. Around two-thirty I had a flat. Then I ran out of gas. I stopped to sleep just before dawn down at the 600-kilometer mark. I slept on the hard-shoulder past a toll booth where a number of truckers had parked to sleep.

Sometime the following afternoon I came across a road accident in the desert. A bus had overturned and been hit by a truck. Dead were laid out by the side of this bus and covered with jackets. Fog off the Pacific drifted over the road. The Indians started to wail as I approached.

All afternoon I was stopped and taxed by police or army. Just after dark I arrived on the crowded, bustling outskirts of Lima. My rear left tire had now worn right through the casing to the wire mesh underneath. I needed to find new wheel studs, new brake pads, new piston rings, a couple of new tires, a part or two for the steering gear. And I had a day to do it. I called Lenny.

'Asshole, where the hell are you?' Lenny asked.

'Lima,' I said.

'What are you doing in Lima?'

'Why don't you come down to Peru and we'll dr—'

'No. You do the rest on your own, pal. See you when you get back to the city.'

Lenny put the phone down.

Two days later I set off. The car wasn't fixed properly. I couldn't get the piston rings done, the front brakes were more of the same types I'd had made up in Quito, the steering mechanism had been tightened but not replaced, a new tire had cost 140 dollars . . .

It was a fourteen-hour drive down the Pan-American highway to Arequipa, a small town nestling in the foothills of the Andes. The road across the Andes started behind the city dump. It was a one-lane dirt track. I started driving up, leaving Arequipa behind me about nine in the morning.

There were no signs and no people, but there were llamas. I saw my first pair of long-necked furry beasts of burden coming past some glacial-looking lakes a couple of hours later. I stopped, got out, wrapped up against the cold and walked over to pet one and take a snap.

Way up on a sand plain, in a sand storm, the road disappeared entirely. Little miniature cyclones whirled over the landscape. As it got dark, the road finally began to descend through a series of green valleys and lakes. I had seen two trucks in ten hours. I pulled into a town around seven that night and was so pleased to see human life at the army checkpoint that I offered cigarettes and cassettes without being asked.

The hearse had definitely blown some rings. It now pulled only on six cylinders. I parked at the end of the square by an open restaurant. I hadn't eaten all day. I went inside. The restaurant was run by a family and had about ten rough wood tables. Chickens were roasting on a spit over a fire. I sat at a table.

Sitting at another table was a group of three unshaven, overweight, middle-aged men in blue uniforms. I ordered chicken. The men invited themselves on to my table. They wanted to know who I was, where I had come from, where I was going and how much Spanish I spoke. I gave them answers but they didn't believe me. They asked the same questions again. I told them the same answers. One of them then had the inspired view that I was a spy.

I went to the car and returned with my strongbox where I kept all my documents. I showed my passport, my license and the title of the car. I showed them all the countries I had driven through and I told them again that I was on my way to the carnaval in Rio. They asked me if I was going to sell the car in Peru. I told them I had no intention of doing so. I loved my car. They asked me how much I paid for the car. I told them. One of them asked if he could buy the hearse off me for 3000 dollars in cash. I thanked him for his most generous offer, but said it was late and if the gentlemen wouldn't mind I had to get going.

They said it was very dangerous driving alone at night. Many, many bandits. Very easy to get the throat cut. I thanked them for their concern. They insisted we go for a drink, the four of us, and talk. I said I was very tired, I'd just driven non-stop from Lima. They said I didn't have a choice in the matter.

I pulled up outside a bar and parked. It was shut. All the lights were extinguished. They got out, banged on the door, woke up the bar-owner and told her we were coming in to drink. The bar-owner was wearing a robe and slippers. She didn't complain, probably because she was used to it. She turned on the lights and opened the door.

Luckily, the men had the alcohol-tolerance level of fleas. After they'd made me buy them each two beers, they were slapping me on the back asking me about green cards and writing out their addresses so that I could keep in touch with them when I got back to New York. One hour later I was allowed to leave. One asked me for a little *regalo*. I asked him what kind of present. He wanted an Elton John cassette. I went down to the car and came back with the three bowls we used to rest our nuts in. I told them they were ceremonial Mexican drinking bowls. I paid the bill. They raised their new bowls, and toasted my good health.

The next morning I crossed into Bolivia. Nobody cared if I had a *libreta* or not. It cost me two dollars.

51

Bolivian TV has a fantastic joke. It concerns this incredible new road system they are in the process of installing in the country. 'El País Avanza! Bolivia!' It goes on showing you this shot of a beautiful super-highway. 'Lo Mejor Que Tenemos!' But the fun part is they're not *built* yet. This is just to let the people know that there *are* great roads but they are in a part of the country nobody can get to. The roads I drove on the first six hours out of La Paz a day-and-a-half later were in parts mud or hardpack. I'd had the car fixed again (as well as was possible). Road-building equipment – earth-movers, dump-trucks, diggers – was in use in some places, but the track from La Paz to Catacoche was bleak alti-plano, hardly anything anywhere, a few llamas, no dwellings, no bars, no country clubs and no tarmac, just mud. The place was wilder, emptier and bleaker than anywhere I had ever been in my limited experience as a tourist, and I kept thinking, this is where my trusty car is going to throw in the towel. This is where we're going to get stuck, outside some tin mine; stay there about a week until the next car or truck comes through, with nothing to eat but that vacu-packed kielbaasa sausage given to me by my dear grandma at Christmas.

In the late afternoon the mud tracks deepened with the rains. The wind howled. It was grey and cold and night fell quickly. The hearse crawled slowly up one empty mountain track after another. Around eight at night I came out of an empty mountain pass and saw, a couple of valleys over, the lights of trucks, a long line of them, parked two-abreast. A Bolivian truck-stop. After eight hours on bleak, muddy roads this ragbag cluster of lean-tos run by Indian women was sanctuary. I'd been wondering for hours if I was on the right road and then I found this, high in the Andes. There were tables and chairs by small improvised kitchens lit by hurricane lamps swinging in the cold wind. There were pots of hot soup cooking over open fires stoked with twigs and sticks. There were maybe twenty different food stalls where the Bolivian truckers, a lot thinner, smaller and fitter than their American counterparts, sat and ate their meager dinners (no $4.99 all-you-can-eat specials down here). The men were tired and dirty from the constant maintenance their trucks required. They ate in silence. I chose a stall and sat at a chair behind a wind-break, just as two truckers were leaving their table.

The old lady fed me with chicken and a root vegetable and a Coke. Then I went to my car and had a snooze.

A trucker told me it was downhill to Catacoche, then one more range of mountains before the Amazon Basin, but the rains had started and he didn't know how long the road would stay open.

'What road's this?' I asked, because I hadn't seen one for about a week.

Four in the morning, after surfing downhill through mud slides and flooded roads, with the windshield wipers going furiously, I started to notice something beautiful. Jungle. Everywhere. Jungle is good for a number of reasons; principally it means you're no longer in the Andes. I wound my window down. The air was warm, not cold. I had no idea where I was but it didn't matter. The rains had now stopped, the track was dry and hard, not running with mud. Just in case I was getting a little too optimistic about making Santa Cruz for lunch, I had another flat. But even that wasn't too unpleasant. Lying in the dirt searching for a spot under the leaf spring for the bottle jack at four in the morning, with a rock laid over the accelerator to stop the engine from stalling, I was content. It was hot. I sweated as I worked changing the wheel. I hadn't sweated since Arequipa.

52

Santa Cruz is an old bandit town which prospered immensely with the booming cocaine and forestry trades of the 1970s and 1980s. My hearse was kind enough to break down right outside a brand-new Toyota dealership – TAME LTDA. I was Señor Wichtendahl's first customer. When he and his son discovered I had driven all the way from New York City they insisted I meet a good friend of theirs, Ken, from Texas. I was tired, dirty, keen to find a hotel for the night and get a freight ride to the border organized, but they insisted (there is a train service which ferries cars to the border. No one knew if there was a road system or not. On the map they showed a road. But you can't trust Bolivian maps.) So while Señor Wichtendahl's mechanics set to work on the hearse we went crosstown, through the narrow sunny, warm streets of Santa Cruz, to meet Ken in a bar on the main square.

I stopped for one drink, which turned into four, then lunch, which moved into cocktails, then dinner, then more cocktails. Ken was an extraordinary character. Finding an old American down in Bolivia because he wanted to be in Bolivia, not because he was posted to Bolivia as part of the DEA or CIA or any other government agency busy interfering down here, piqued my curiosity. But Ken was an anarchist and you're a lot safer being an anarchist in Bolivia than the United States. Ken came down to Bolivia as part of a civil engineering team in the 1950s. He met his future wife Esther, had a brief affair, then returned to the States. Back in the States he realized that Bolivia had given him a new perspective on freedom and personal liberty. There were far too many laws in the United States, so he moved back to Bolivia, married Esther and had stayed ever since. Bolivia, he told me, was crooked as hell but he preferred it. He told me a couple of Bolivian justice stories. The first was of an incident that had occurred a few days earlier, a shooting on the street just around the corner from where we sat. The victim was a twenty-five-year-old squirt who owed an old man in town money. For months this old man had asked the kid for his money but the kid kept blowing him off, one excuse after the other, until the old man's patience snapped. He gets his gun and goes out looking for the kid. It just so happens the first day he's out looking the kid comes strolling down the street toward him. The old man asks the kid for his money. The kid doesn't have it and taunts the old man. The old man shoots him. Problem is the man doesn't have his glasses on, he can't see very well, so when he shoots him he can only wing the little runt. The kid drops to the floor screaming, crawls under the nearest car and hides. The old man leans over on his walking-stick, then empties the chamber of his gun under the car and kills him. The police are called. The police know all about it and they don't like the kid any more than the old man does, but they have to do something. So they put the old man under arrest, take him down to the jailhouse and lock him up for the night. But the next day they say that provided he agrees to return to the jail at six every evening to sleep the night in his cell, he can go free. The old man thinks this is pretty damned fair. He walks out of the jailhouse, spends his days doing whatever he was doing before, and then returns to sleep in his cell at night. This goes on for a week or two by which time the fuss over the shooting has died down and the public have got something new to talk about – the election race between Banzer and Goni. The police now say to the old man: listen, don't bother coming back any more, you've been inconvenienced enough. Go home. You're a free man. 'And that,' said Ken, 'is Bolivian justice at its best.'

'Where are the disadvantages?'

Second justice story. Ken and his wife were burgled the week before. The thieves stripped their house of all the consumer durables – TV, video, stereo – but Esther is quite sure the crooks were working with the police – they normally do down in Santa Cruz. So when the police officer arrives at the house to file a report on all the items stolen, Esther tags on the end of the list the sum of 5000 dollars in cash. When the officer leaves the house, Ken asks his wife why she just told the man all that money was stolen when it wasn't. Esther explains that there is no chance anybody will be caught, but at least this way someone will be punished. The police will now assume the thieves had taken the five grand but not *declared* it. When questioned about this money they will naturally deny any knowledge of it. The police will then give them a good beating for taking them for fools.

'Which is fine,' Ken added with a grin. 'As long as you got insurance up the ass.'

53

The freight yard on the outskirts of Santa Cruz was submerged in about two feet of mud when I took the hearse down to put it up on the *lancha* I had rented – a flat-car to carry it for the next twenty-six hours. I didn't want to leave the hearse in the yard overnight, so I slept in it. At first light an engine shunted the *lancha* up and down the tracks to join a long line of box-cars being assembled for the run to the border. There were no passenger carriages on this train but there were passengers: a couple of young soldiers, a group of young students brought to the yard by a convoy of four-wheel vehicles, two young Indians, and a strange-looking European with a florid face, plus-fours, walking boots, thick socks, a long-sleeved cotton shirt, and a small back pack.

I watched him stride through the muddy yard at seven in the morning from the roof of the box-car, the next carriage down from my *lancha*, where I had decided to sit. The roof of the rust-colored box-cars offered the best view of the country. I planned on spending the day up on the roof. The European joined the train further down, then climbed inside a box-car out of the sun.

At nine the train finally pulled out of the yard. The parents waved to the kids, the kids waved back and a gathering of characters now sat on the *lancha* on the limited floor space to the front and rear of the hearse. A man with some chickens put them under the front wheels, two young soldiers sat in two off-road tires they had bought, Indian women with full ankle-length skirts and bundles of belongings sat next to them.

The train built up speed. The movement on the roof was a lot more violent than I had anticipated. I watched the sleepers rush past fifteen feet below and soon realized I could not move without being thrown off. For a half-hour I sat and gripped the single hand-hold on the roof and kicked myself for not thinking about how fast the train might go. The train sped into the flat green countryside of high grass, past the Menonite soya farms under a big, blustery sky, and after some time slowed. The movement on the roof became less pronounced. I got up, walked across the roof to the ladder at the end and descended. From the base of the ladder I could hop across to the *lancha*. Once on it I edged round the hearse to the box-car in the rear. I climbed up on to the roof of this one which had much better hand-holds than the car I'd been sitting on. I spent the rest of the morning watching the country pass by, feeling the fresh, warm breeze on my face and experiencing a great deal of simple pleasure watching the Bolivian road system disappear in thick undergrowth by the side of the track, or slide under two feet of water and mud. This was the only road to the border according to the map I'd bought from the automobile club in La Paz and there was no chance the hearse would have made it through 500 miles of it.

When the children in the villages saw the long train coming they would run and wave. Everybody waved, even the dour-looking Menonites in overalls and black felt hats working with their hoes. I waved too. I was almost in Brazil.

Around twelve we pulled into a little station with no name. I saw people get off the *lancha* and run to a little *cantina* nearby. I climbed down and ran over too. I wanted food and drink. The girl in the *cantina* was very slow. While I was being served the train started to pull out. The girl was slow because she knew we all had to be on the train and the train didn't wait for anybody. I ran off before she could give me change.

In the afternoon, a couple of young Indians came up on the roof to sit next to me. The boys got off the train just before sunset. When night came, the stars came out and I liked it immensely. I was on my own for a while, looking up at the stars, when a voice said, 'Hi there! Speak English?'

It was the European.

'I do.'

'Mind if I join you?'

'Be my guest.'

He came up and sat with his legs dangling over the end of the carriage. He said he suffered in the sun because of his complexion, but this was certainly the best place to be. He introduced himself as Anthony. Anthony was an Englishman by birth but a Raelite by choice. Raelites, he explained, are followers of the prophet Rael who believe we are all descended from extra-terrestrials. Bolivia, he informed me, was an area of tremendous extra-terrestrial activity. Did I know this?

I did not.

'It is.'

He asked me if I believed in extra-terrestrials. I said I'd never seen one. He said they are *every*where. Which was why he and his friends were building an embassy for them in Tel Aviv. It was going to be a reception area for when they returned to earth.

'They *are* going to come, you know,' he told me. 'Soon.'

I watched shooting stars. Anthony watched for extra-terrestrials. It started to get cold. At nine I said I was going to bed.

'Well, cheerio,' he said. I got up and walked over the roof and climbed down the ladder to my *lancha*. The train rattled along in the dark. I inched along the side, opened the door and slid inside where it was still warm from the heat of the day. I lay on my futon and thought: it's almost finished now. And as I thought about that I realized I was quite happy to go home now. It was the first time I had looked forward to it since leaving.

Sometime during the night I was woken when the train pulled into a small town and there was a banging on the car roof.

'Policía! Narco! Abre la puerta!'

I unlocked a door. Four rough-looking plain-clothesmen searched the car by flashlight, then demanded cassettes and cigarettes.

At first light we came to a small town and stopped. The Raelite was nowhere to be seen, the soldier had gone, so had the women. There were two new people on the *lancha* in the morning, a scrawny, dark-haired man with a mustache and a sweater with a pattern of German crosses, and a middle-aged Bolivian with white tennis shoes, a wind-breaker and gold Ray-Ban aviators who stood on the roof of the box-car ahead, like a sentinel on duty, upright, arms crossed.

I went with the scrawny man to the *cantina* by the station house. I bought two *empanadas* and a liter of Coca-Cola. The man bought six live chickens. The legs of the chickens were trussed together but they flapped and squawked, and it was too much of a handful. He gave me two to carry. We ran along the railway embankment, passed the chickens up to a man on the *lancha*, and scrambled aboard. At three in the afternoon, the train pulled into the freight yard at Corumba.

54

Carnaval is the big mother of all hoolies. Seven long days and nights of around-the-clock dancing, drinking, fighting, fucking, fireworks, floats, costumes, samba bands, soca schools, celebrity parties, block parties, house parties, street parties, roof parties, private parties, beach parties, bar crawls. And when it was over, when the legions of street cleaners descended on the littered streets to sweep aside the rice, the broken beer bottles, the discarded items of clothing; when the bands and the dancers had finally stumbled home, like any good party there were still isolated cells of the die-hard on the streets or the city beaches; half-naked, eyes popping out of their skulls, holding on to complete strangers and waving to the good viewers back home. It was an amazing event. I watched it all on the TV in my room at a little hotel on the Pantanel, sick in the stomach and sick in the head at having missed the whole week of festivities after all that driving, arguing, bribing and hustling. It was terrible ...

A week later I was well again and back on the road. The time had now come to cast an eye homeward. This upset me. On the drive to São Paulo and Rio I could hardly concentrate on the stunning road system they had installed in this country (a two-lane blacktop. No holes. White dividing lines. Signposts. Regular truck-stops); my thoughts were elsewhere. When I pulled up outside my hotel on Copacabana Beach the next day, I turned the motor off and sat and listened to the old boy with a heavy heart as he whirred and banged and popped until he finally expired with a shake and a wheeze. We were there now, our final destination, and I was going to have to sell my car because I couldn't afford to ship him home. It broke my heart.

At the front desk there was a note waiting for me: 'In the bar, you bugger. Tarris.'

I went to the bar. No girls with shoes with bows on their toes. It was carpet and chrome and quite civilized.

Tarris was sitting on a bar-stool reading a palm when I walked up.

'Two children?'

'No!'

'Three?'

She got up and walked off.

I walked over. Tarris looked up and grinned.

'Welcome and what fucking took you?'

55

Two days later we drove to the airport. A friend of Tarris's in Colombia had given him an engineering job over in Venezuela. He had tried calling us in Cali to inform us of his sudden change of plans but he couldn't find us. So he flew to Caracas and called Lenny back in Brooklyn. Lenny had told him where I would be staying in Rio. Now he was here to finish his holiday and look for some new business opportunities before returning home to the quiet life in Cornwall. He was going to stay on a little longer and persuaded me to let him use the car during the time of his stay, then he promised to sell it to a reputable morgue when he left.

We parked outside the terminal. I fetched my bag from the

rear and closed the door. I stood back and admired him for the last time. He was muddy and dusty; his front end was banged, so were the wheel-skirts. Only one tire was still a whitewall. All the hubcaps had fallen off. On the rear window one of the kids up in Puno, back in Peru, had written in the thick dust: 'Drahcoola.' And as I stood there looking at him for the last time, I remembered the day I went out to Queens to buy him –

'Come, on, bunje. Let's go.'

– and I remembered that first night driving with Lenny down to New Orleans –

'Bar's open. Ein for the strasse?'

– and the night in a graveyard in Mexico when Tarris was sleeping in the back and he woke up terrified, convinced a ghost was trying to castrate him. So much to remember.

I gave Tarris my camera.

'Take one picture of us together, please,' I said. Then I stood up against the front deck and put on my best face. The camera clicked.

In the airport bar we reminisced a little more. That time a young lady in Colombia put her tongue up Tarris's nose and said, 'Umm! Coca!'

Then the flight was called.

Epilogue

Six weeks later I was back in New York City engaged in the peace process, trying to mollify the various agencies I owed large amounts of money to, and it was not going well, when the phone rang...

It was long-distance, from Brazil.

'Tarris, you rapscallion,' I said, 'what a pleasant surprise. I was just thinking about you. Did you sell my beasty?'

Tarris changed the subject with skill and launched into a filthy story of a recent misadventure in Brazil with a young teacher of the Lambada from Bahia that made me hoot with laughter.

'Disgusting,' I said. 'But I need money. Did you sell the car?'

'Ehm, not yet, bunje.'

'Oh. Why not?'

'I'll call you this evening and explain *every*thing. But first things first. D'you think you could do me a big favor . . . ?'

Then he explained himself. A container-load of Brazilian surfboards was waiting at the docks in Jersey. He had bought the boards cheap and wanted to sell them in the United States and England and make some money. He wanted me to go down to the docks and make sure these surfboards were not damaged in transit.

I was not thrilled with this idea but I agreed to do it and that afternoon I went out to Jersey. As usual it took a couple of hours at the docks to get anyone to show me the container. But when the doors swung open I was stunned.

There were no surfboards inside. Just one large, dusty old car with a big ribbon of rope around it.

I slithered down the side of the rusty container. On the roof, attached to the ribbon was a little red shoe with a bow on the toe and a note in the heel.

'Couldn't bring myself to sell it. Pay me back when you can. Your friend, Tarris.'

Acknowledgements

During the writing of this work the author was lucky enough to find support, friendship and often a roof for long periods of time. To the following I am deeply indebted: Johnny, Chris and Steff; Eva, Lynn and Danny; Anna; my own family; and most of all my beautiful wife-to-be, Gemma, who was patient and long-suffering and always there for me. Always.

Thank you.